Books:
Buyers and Borrowers

Books:
Buyers and Borrowers

Peter H. Mann

ANDRE DEUTSCH

FIRST PUBLISHED 1971 BY
ANDRE DEUTSCH LIMITED
105 GREAT RUSSELL STREET
LONDON WCI

COPYRIGHT © 1971 BY PETER H. MANN
ALL RIGHTS RESERVED

PRINTED IN GREAT BRITAIN BY
TONBRIDGE PRINTERS LTD
TONBRIDGE KENT

ISBN 0 233 96292 1

Contents

The author's royalties on the sales of this book are being given to the Charter Group of the Booksellers Association.

Introduction

This is the second book based on studies into social aspects of book reading assisted by a research grant made by the Booksellers Association of Great Britain and Ireland. The initial grant for the academic year 1967–68 was extended for a further two years after some of the early results of the research had been considered.

The present book is largely a report on work which was carried out in 1967–68 but either not analysed or written up in time for the first book, or work actually carried out and analysed during the second year's research. The reader of this book will find it useful to have read the first book,[1] but the present book is self-contained and does not require reference to the first one.

The first book presented a sociological 'model' which had been developed to try to help look more systematically at the very complex types and functions of adult books. This model is reproduced on page 9 so that it can again be considered in the light of greater experience of the problems of researching into books. In general it has continued to be helpful in considering books in special ways. It is very clear that there is now little to be gained from attempting to study 'books' in one gross category. There are numerous ways of interpreting the word 'book' and this word can mean different things to different people. What is now clearly needed is the kind of book reading

[1] *Books and Reading*, André Deutsch, London, 1969.

research which will deal with books in realistic categories according to the functions which they fulfil for the readers. The model begins with a 'work-leisure' continuum which then divides into three main divisions of 'utilitarian', 'social' and 'personal' reading. Whilst the three main categories cannot always be discrete (for example, a biography could be a popular best seller and also invaluable in an academic course) the divisions do help to distinguish between the general functions of books and these distinctions then help in considering how people will actually *use* the books, whether or not personal possession is likely to be important, what place borrowing will have in the scheme of things, and how books may be considered as gifts.

Consideration of these factors in the hypothetical model has helped in looking at areas in which research could be carried out. One important point is the way in which people come to learn about books. The world of books is one in which the relationship between producer and consumer is very different from that of many other products. An annual output of over 30,000 new books in this country alone presents an information problem of the first magnitude and one which greatly concerns publishers and booksellers who want their potential customers to be aware of what is available. Yet along with this problem there must also be seen the interesting fact that books are virtually the only commodity which is given the free publicity accorded in the book review pages of newspapers and magazines, albeit that the bulk of the books dealt with in reviews are of 'literary' or 'academic' interest. The various ways in which different sorts of books attract

A SOCIOLOGICAL MODEL FOR THE ANALYSIS OF LEISURE BOOK READING

WORK ← 'UTILITARIAN' READING ← Extrinsic		'SOCIAL' READING — Books reviewed and recommended by opinion leaders		'PERSONAL' READING — Intrinsic → → LEISURE
Work books / Texts Manuals Reference books	Home manuals and reference / Cookery Car manuals Guides Hobbies	← Self-improvement → Non-fiction / History Biography Memoirs Travel	Fiction / 'Good' novels	Distraction / Romances Mystery Detective
		Status conferring books		Only inverted status
For reference only		May be read and re-read		Read once
Buy to have at hand Borrow to extend knowledge Buy good ones previously borrowed Buy as gifts		Buy or borrow for self. Perhaps buy after reading borrowed copy Buy as present if recipient's taste known, but status present anyway	Buy as present only if recipient's tastes very well known	Buy paperbacks Borrow from library or friend 'Throwaway', Doubtful as present
		Challenge the reader's attitudes and beliefs		Reinforce the reader's attitudes and beliefs

9

people's attention seemed to be worthy of study and so Chapter 1 is devoted to this topic.

The model also distinguishes the way in which people acquire books and general surveys of books and reading have often pointed to the fact that books appear to be popular as gifts. This diffusion of books by present-giving seemed another aspect of the book world which had not been considered and it seemed desirable to attempt to find ways in which it could be researched. This was not easy, but it was possible to gain some insights from a question-naire enquiry of people (albeit self-selected volunteers) who had received books as Christmas gifts, and to look rather more systematically at book token purchases and encash-ments since these are a clear form of book gift substitutes.

A further point of great importance in the use of books, and again something virtually unique to books, is the way in which readers may obtain books. In Britain we have what many people consider to be the finest public library system in the world. Whilst no public service is free (and 'free' services such as health and education may be very expensive to the community as a whole), the public library service in this country has few equals in making available to the borrower virtually any book which may be requested. As one London librarian recently reported at a conference on libraries and the book trade, a review in the Sunday papers resulted in 300 demands for a new novel the very next day, and a total of 800 within a week. Such demands upon a public library system reflect an interesting expectation of a high quality of service and also a strong disinclination to make a personal purchase of a book costing 30s. in its case-bound form. It is clear, therefore, that the buying and borrowing of books is important to everyone concerned with books, from the university lecturer trying to encourage and advise his students how best to spend their £38 annual budget of books and stationery, right across to the public librarian catering for the marginal book user who may only rarely feel the need of a book at all. A good part of the research work in this second year was devoted to looking at this complex problem of buying and borrowing and distinguishing the types of people who do buy and who do borrow, and these are dealt with in Chapters 3 and 4.

The model gave the name 'personal reading' to categories of light fiction, often published mainly in paperback form, which may be regarded as escapism, distraction reading or 'leisure' of the simplest kind. Since the types of books which come into this category generally fall outside the more 'literary' category of books which receive reviews in newspapers and magazines their readers are all too easily ignored. Yet it is clear that for many people the light fiction paperback has a very real function in providing for their leisure and may well be the main contact they have with books. Research in this field is not easy, but it is important not to sweep aside this category of books and readers simply because they do not come up to the necessary social and intellectual standards required for entry into the more exclusive world of 'culture' as exemplified by the books and readers catered for by the review columns. Chapter 5 on light fiction looks at the reading of light fiction in an objective way so as to understand the part it contributes to the total world of books, and details gained in a study of readers of romantic novels are given to illustrate some of the misconceptions that may be held about such readers.

It can be seen, then, that the second year of work into books and reading continued the use of the sociological model as a guide to areas for study but that there are still vast areas awaiting research. The concluding chapter attempts to draw together some of the threads which run through the year's studies and indicates some of the many questions which not only are still unanswered, but as yet require a clearer formulation.

In all our work my research assistant (Miss Jacqueline Burgoyne) and I have continued to be greatly indebted to publishers, booksellers and librarians for their interest and willing cooperation. Mr Peter Stockham, the managing director of Dillon's University Bookshop, has continued as the chairman of the liaison committee with the Booksellers Association and his unfailing support and encouragement has been invaluable. The headquarters staff at the Booksellers Association have continued with their unobtrusive administrative assistance and we again thank them for their cooperation. The moving spirit in gaining support for the continuance of this research for a further two years was Mr Eric Bailey, managing director of H. J. Lear's of Cardiff, who by the time this book is published will be the President of the Booksellers Association of Great Britain and Ireland. In token of our appreciation of his encouragement to us and recognising his devotion to the world of books we dedicate this book to him.

PETER H. MANN
Sheffield, June, 1969.

Chapter 1

Books and the Public

Introduction

In this chapter we consider how the general public is made aware of books. We shall deal with various means by which the potential reading public (which we consider to be all literate people) has its attention drawn to the fact that books exist and that books can fill a place in people's lives.

One of the major difficulties in informing the public about books is the enormous number of them that exist. It is estimated that there are now in Britain approximately a quarter of a million titles in print and that about 23,000 new titles (excluding reprints and new editions) are published each year. Clearly every publisher, bookseller and librarian would like to have his potential buyer or borrower well informed about the wide variety of books available, but the very size of the available stock of titles can intimidate would-be readers. The wealth of provision of children's books (about 2,000 new titles a year) does not overcome the ignorance of many Christmas or birthday present book buyers. Adults with little or no knowledge of modern children's writers tend to buy the 'safe' and frequently quite dull children's 'classics' because they know the titles or authors and what is known is reassuring. Apart from the relative cheapness of many editions of children's 'classics' which makes them seem a 'good buy', the unsophisticated adult buyer selects a name or title which he or she knew as a child and this makes the whole operation at least a generation out of date. This particular example demonstrates how people choose books for purchase (or for borrowing) from very narrow ranges. This chapter is concerned with the ways in which 'books' are brought to the attention of 'people', and for this analysis we must discriminate between the various types of books, the various potential readers and the media used by publishers, booksellers and librarians.

If reference is made to the model (p. 9) it can be seen that different sorts of books are used for different sorts of purposes and so it must be recognised at the outset that highly technical books of high standard may have only a limited circle of potential users. For instance, a book such as *Crystals and the Polarizing Microscope*, now in its 4th edition, is obviously an established standard text for a fairly clearly distinguishable group of students and staff in higher education; to attempt to draw the attention of the whole reading public to this book would be a pointless exercise. On the other hand a new practical book on cookery or gardening could appeal to thousands of people and different tactics would be called for in publicising such books. Light fiction, especially in paperback form, is often regarded as 'impulse' selection and attention may therefore be given by publishers to jacket design and visual stimuli which may catch the browser's eye; spines may have special colours which tell the reader that this is a Gollancz yellow back detective or thriller or a red and yellow back Mills & Boon romance. In the category of 'social' reading which deals with those books, both fiction and non-fiction, which are considered as 'literature' there is an interesting group which receives a lot of attention from reviewers in general newspapers and periodicals. These are books which, whilst they are sometimes called 'best sellers', are frequently books which only enjoy a passing success but by changing week by week or month by month, they provide 'news' for the various media of communication and enable the literary pundits to have something new to write or talk about. No journalist or broadcaster could make a success of a column or half-hour programme which had to deal with the continued good sales of a primer in Latin grammar or wide-selling thrillers or romances which are hardly distinguishable from each other. The literary world is a world of 'culture' in which new ideas and viewpoints are continuously sought by both writers and readers and it is the world of intellectual thought which marks off 'literature' from 'light' reading. Yet the literary world tends to stop short of actual expertise which becomes exclusive; the *general* review columns of the quality press normally review only those books which would be regarded as comprehensible for the reasonably intelligent *lay* reader. Specialist books are dealt with by specialist reviewers in specialist journals; it is only now and then that a well-written book for the specialist is readable enough to make a hit with the general public.

These introductory paragraphs demonstrate how a number of factors must operate, at times in quite complex relationships with each other, in making potential readers aware of books that are available to them. Let us then, before proceeding further with the analysis, consider some of these factors.

I. PEOPLE LEARN ABOUT BOOKS IN DIFFERENT WAYS, BUT ALL THEIR LEARNING IS THROUGH SEEING OR HEARING, OR COMBINATIONS OF THESE TWO SENSES

(a) People *see* books in bookshops and other types of 'retail outlets', in libraries, at some forms of work and in homes.

(b) People *read* about books in newspapers, magazines, journals and other books. Books may be reviewed by supposedly impartial reviewers and they may be advertised by the publishers in more partisan fashion. But besides books as books, they may also be items of news (especially if a book becomes the centre of a well-publicised legal case such as *Lady Chatterley's Lover* or *Last Exit to Brooklyn*) and people may thus read about books because of their 'news value'.

(c) People *hear* about books. A great deal of this form of learning comes in an informal way through conversations with other people, which may range from comments on the worth of a new book on concrete made by one civil engineer to another right across to the cocktail hour gossip about a stimulating new novel written by a completely unknown author. Informal discussions are virtually impossible to survey systematically, but many publishers and reviewers believe that informal talk can influence the success of a new novel. More formal ways in which people hear about books may be illustrated by the programmes about books put out by the BBC. Television, which caters primarily for the mass audience, gives very little serious attention to books as books (as against books as news), but sound radio, which caters more for minorities and specialists, has both review programmes for new books and talks about particular books. It should not be over-looked that in using specially produced books to link with instructional and educational programmes on both radio and television the BBC is itself an important publisher.

(d) People *receive advertising* about books. Whilst it may be said that this is really a form of reading about books, it is worth while separating this rather special aspect and dealing with it as a category in itself. In section (b) we briefly referred to general advertising of books in news-papers, magazines, journals and so on. Very little specialised advertising goes into general newspapers or magazines because the costs could not be justified. Academic books may be advertised in specialist journals, but clearly not all such books are, otherwise journals would contain much more advertising than they do, and some academic journals contain very little advertising indeed. In recent years there has been a great development in what may be called 'direct mailing' of advertising matter, and this is a much more systematic way of catching the attention of people who are likely to be interested in specialist books by concentrating the advertising on chosen groups. This operation may be organised for different types of people and with interest questionnaires completed at an early stage by recipients, as in the case of the University Mailing Service organisation. It may be done in less systematic ways from chosen lists of addresses as appears sometimes to be the case with sellers of pornography, at times with results distressing to the recipients. Generally speaking, however, direct advertising concentrates on informing specialists of all kinds about books which might interest them. It is widely used at all levels of education and is important also in medicine and other technological subjects.

2. PUBLISHERS, BOOKSELLERS AND LIBRARIANS USE DIFFERENT MEANS TO DRAW THE ATTENTION OF PEOPLE TO BOOKS

(a) A distinction can be made between *advertising* and *publicity* for books.[1] Advertising may be regarded as direct action, normally costing money, taken to draw the attention of people to books. Thus advertising of particular books in a newspaper or bookshop, posters, cards and other display material, direct mailing to selected people and much of the work of publishers' representatives is to do with advertising. Bookshops and libraries do not engage in advertising to the extent that publishers do, but when booksellers use the advertising material supplied by publishers and when public libraries put on special displays of books on a particular topic (hobbies, holidays, foreign languages etc.) or compile printed lists of recently published books they are, in their way, advertising. By contrast, publicity is a more subtle and less direct way of drawing attention to books. In its extreme form it may be defined as attention given to books which costs nothing to the publicity seeker. Thus a highly publicised divorce case involving an author may draw attention to his writing and could result in people being interested in his work.

[1] I am grateful to Mr Michael Hyde of William Collins Ltd., for this useful distinction.

For a book to be considered obscene, especially if the publishers are charged in courts of law, can produce a lot of publicity, though this can be costly if the publishers are found guilty. Recently Gore Vidal was able to gain publicity when W. H. Smith's, the booksellers, declined to stock one of his novels on their shelves (to name the book here would be to add to this free publicity, so we will leave it unnamed!). In the ideal-type form of publicity the attention drawn to the book should cost nothing, but clearly this is to rely overmuch upon fortuitous circumstances, and publishers' publicity departments attempt to achieve publicity at low cost. The most obvious and generally recognised form is by supplying review copies of books to various newspapers, magazines and journals. Here the cost of the book, at production price, plus postage, is all that is invested. However, the publisher cannot expect that every copy sent out will be reviewed (and many are not) and, most important of all, the reviews may be quite damning. The publisher cannot control what the reviewer writes about his book and he must, to some degree, gamble that the book will be well reviewed or else that even a poor review is better than no review. We shall consider this point in some detail a little later on. Other forms of publicity may be gained by means such as press releases or press conferences about new books. Here the emphasis is frequently on the topicality of a book or the fame of an author. In April 1970, Professor Christiaan Barnard, the heart surgeon, was widely reported upon and photographed with his second wife at a press conference at the Dorchester Hotel to 'launch' his autobiography. His publishers later announced that the book and its author had received pre-publication press coverage of 7,325 single-column inches and post-publication reviews and comment amounting to 3,647 column inches by mid-April, and they wondered if this was a record. Authors who arouse great general interest, such as Sir Alec Rose or Robin Knox-Johnson, may find themselves involved in quite exhausting tours of public appearances, lunches, dinners, press conferences, radio and television interviews and so on, all promoted by the publishers. Here the line between direct advertising and publicity frequently becomes blurred. An interesting innovation in publicity for books has been seen in recent short speaking tours made by small groups of authors (mainly novelists) which have received sponsorship from the Arts Council of Great Britain. These 'meet the author' trips have brought together writers, readers, teachers, pupils and all sorts of people, utilising bookshops, libraries and schools as meeting places. Clearly neither authors nor publishers 'plug' their own goods, but it would be illogical to expect interest in a writer's works not to be increased. A more commercial form combining advertising and publicity is the 'literary luncheon'. Here it is conventional to have a number of authors present, though any one lunch may focus on the publication of one, usually famous, author's new book. The general public who attend such gatherings pay quite highly for the food and entertainment they receive, but the cost of supplying speakers and authors is normally met by the publishers.

(b) Books are media of communication between authors and readers, but it is rarely convenient for an author to involve himself in anything beyond the production of a reasonably tidy and accurate typescript form of his communication. Thus the functions of publisher, bookseller and librarian are essential for the diffusion of multiple copies of an author's writings. Relatively few authors can make a living from writing alone and whilst very popular authors such as Agatha Christie may be rumoured to have incomes of around £100,000 a year, incomes of £500 or £600 a year are more common. But publishers and booksellers are commercially involved in books on a full-time basis and to be part-time publishers or booksellers is not easy. What does happen is that publishers tend to diversify their types of books with a view to finding steady sellers in various fields and booksellers may gain income from library supply work, mail orders and even the sale of goods other than books, such as records, stationery and 'fancy goods'. The important point to which this discussion leads is that when the author has convinced a publisher that his book is worth producing the publisher has then to convince the bookseller that it is worth stocking. Of course, every book in a publisher's warehouse is *available* to the public if ordered, but if the bookshop is regarded as a 'showcase' for books likely to attract sales on demand then the relationship between the bookshop-buyer and the publishers' representatives (plus advertising) becomes crucial. Added to this there is the matter of library stocks of books, especially in public libraries. Not only do sales to libraries quite often determine the commercial success or failure of a book, but also the very fact of books being *displayed* in libraries can help to arouse interest in authors and subjects. Thus it should be recognised that, in drawing attention to books, publishers must direct their energies to advertising and publicising books to booksellers and librarians as well as to private buyers. The institutional buyers, especially large libraries, work from different, largely non-commercial principles, since they are usually offering a *service* to readers and in evaluating the service given commercial principles do not usually apply. It may be important for libraries to inform their borrowers of the stock available for lending, but because a particular book is not actually referred to or borrowed more than twice a year it does not necessarily follow that the book is a 'failure'.

At this stage we may now draw together some of the general principles which have been established. Two major propositions have been put forward.

I. POTENTIAL READERS LEARN ABOUT BOOKS THROUGH THE SENSES OF SEEING AND HEARING

This may be shown as:

Seen in	Read about, by way of reviews or direct advertising in publications such as	Heard about in	Received direct information about by
Bookshops Other retail 'outlets' Libraries Homes	Newspapers General magazines Specialist journals	Private conversations Radio programmes Television programmes Cinema adaptations	Specialist direct mailing service General direct mail advertising

2. PUBLISHERS, BOOKSELLERS AND LIBRARIANS USE DIFFERENT MEANS OF COMMUNICATION IN DRAWING PEOPLE'S ATTENTION TO BOOKS AND THE PEOPLE TO WHOM THEY DIRECT THEIR COMMUNICATIONS STAND IN CERTAIN RELATIONSHIPS TO EACH OTHER

This may be shown as:

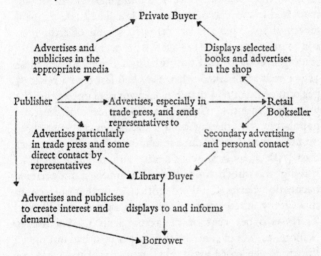

It must be stressed that both the table and the diagram above are simplifications which omit finer detail so as to present general principles. In the following sections of this chapter we deal in detail with some aspects which have been mentioned in the preceding general discussion.

Seeing Books
To the person who is accustomed to having books about him, who uses books for his work and enjoys them during

his leisure time it may seem almost inconceivable that people can live without seeing books. Yet it is not too difficult to exist as an adult in a world where books are rarely seen. Clearly, at school, even for those who leave at the earliest opportunity, it is not possible to avoid some contact with books, ancient and dilapidated though some of these may be, but once schooling has ended, home, work and leisure can easily be bookless. The ERC national survey of 1965[1] gave 31 per cent of a sample of 2,300 men and women aged 16 or over who were not currently reading a book or had not just finished one. When these 31 per cent were asked when they had last read a book 69 per cent of them said that they had not read one within the past three months, which gives 21 per cent of the total population not having read a book for at least three months. In analysis of these results by social class the upper class (AB categories) were nearly all 'readers' and non-reading was much more prevalent amongst the manual occupation classes (C_2DE categories). A further question in this survey asked when people had last visited a library. Thirty-two per cent of the respondents used a library 'seldom' or 'never', and another 21 per cent had not used a library in the past four weeks. Again, non-use was more common amongst manually occupied people than amongst the middle-class people. Another question asked people how many books they had in their home, and whilst many with large numbers of books might find such a question difficult to answer, the survey obtained replies of '20 books or less' from 31 per cent of respondents.

[1] European Research Consultants Ltd., *Report on Books and Reading Habits*, London, 1965.

These results are interesting in that the figure of about one-third was obtained for:

1. People not now reading a book or just having finished one.
2. People who seldom or never use a library.
3. People whose homes contain 20 or fewer books.

It does not follow that a third of the population constitute a homogeneous group who do not read, borrow or own books, since the data of this survey were not analysed to test such a hypothesis. Also the survey did not ask respondents if they had recently been into a bookshop, perhaps because the definition of a 'bookshop' might have been too difficult to agree. Confirmatory figures from other surveys support the general picture of the ERC survey. The Society of Young Publishers' survey of 1959[1] found 36 per cent of their sample owning under 50 books and the Tottenham survey of 1946 (now very out of date) found 30 per cent of the population had never been in the library at all. Stuart, in his survey of three London Boroughs in 1952,[2] concluded that 'less than 60 per cent of the population ever reads a book'. These now dated surveys must be regarded with caution against developments in paperback publishing and greatly extended library lendings in recent years. For example, in the year 1968–69 600 million books were borrowed from public libraries, an increase of nearly 60 per cent on the year 1960–61. Clearly more people are in touch with books than was so in the 1950s,

[1] Society of Young Publishers, 'Books in London', *Books*, Jan.–Feb.' 1959.
[2] A. Stuart, 'Reading Habits in Three London Boroughs', *Journal of Documentation*, Vol. 8, no. 1, 1952.

but equally it would seem that a good minority are still outside the world of books.

The analysis of the geographical distribution of bookshops in Chapter 3 draws attention to the paucity of high-standard bookshops in many parts of the country, and with genuine bookshops so scarce the general public will only see a very restricted selection of books for sale in retail outlets which are basically *not* bookshops but which do sell a limited number of books, frequently only paperback fiction of the lighter type. The general shopper who does not have access to, or does not go into, a shop which sells only or almost wholly books, may well still see a book display of quite a wide range in a branch of W. H. Smith's or Boots the chemists. Both of these chains provide for the sale of books in towns where bookshops *per se* may be few in number or non-existent. But in many small towns or villages, and in many urban areas too, the shop which has a sign outside which includes 'books' amongst 'newspapers, magazines, tobacco, cigarettes, sweets and chocolates' will have only a rack of paperbacks (serviced by the wholesaler's representative) and their proprietors would be astonished if a customer were to ask them to obtain a copy of a recently published historical study selling at 50s. Innocent visitors to the West End of London might at first glance be impressed by the recent increase in the number of bookshops in the Soho area, but closer inspection of the windows under the sign 'Books' would reveal that these are specialists in erotica and pornography, none of whom appear to be members of the Booksellers Association of Great Britain.

When one considers what people *do* see in proper

bookshops and public libraries it is interesting to note how few of these places are laid out so as to attract people inside and to interest people once they are in. In the survey of 115 bookshops previously reported on in *Books and Reading* we found 33 per cent of shop entrances 'uninviting' and 36 per cent of shops with no sign-posting to various sections. Subsequent to this survey during a visit to London, I tried the experiment of pretending to be a foreign visitor to the capital who wanted to see what London's bookshops were like. I 'discovered' that a street called 'Charing Cross Road' seemed to be the main place for bookshops, and, like an assiduous foreign visitor, I started at the southern end and worked my way steadily along, calling in at every shop selling books. Some shops are well known, some are hardly bookshops; some are very small, some are very big. But the general feeling the visitor had at the end of this journey was one of bafflement. If these are a cross-section of what the British call 'bookshops' what ever do the British consider to be books? Particularly in evidence also was the sturdy independence and insularity of the British, in that few concessions appeared to be made to the stranger who might not know where to find what he wanted. There were a few exceptions, but some shops were more like private collections than public shops.

Much more attention is given in libraries to helping customers to find their way about, and it is a poor public library whose general layout cannot be worked out in a few minutes from the labelling of sections and shelves by the casual visitor. It is customary for fiction to be separated from non-fiction and for all fiction to be shelved alphabetically by author. If a classification such as the Dewey decimal system is used for non-fiction then all books are shelved in a known order, though some libraries may set aside special shelves outside the Dewey classification for fiction and popular non-fiction categories such as 'biography' or 'travel'. The Dewey system is based on a division of all books into ten main categories, the basic divisions being numbered 0 to 9 and these numbers are the first of three specialist digit groups which can then extend to several decimals. Thus 300 is the group of the social sciences, 301 is sociology, 301.36 is urban sociology. The main groupings are:

0 General	5 Pure Sciences
1 Philosophy	6 Applied Sciences
2 Religion	7 Arts and amusements
3 Social Sciences	8 Literature
4 Philology	9 History and geography

The public library has the great advantage over the bookshop that it does not have to try to get rid of its books as quickly as possible because of economic pressures. One result is that, in the public library, all books may be considered to be of equal merit and none has to be 'pushed' because of topicality or stocked in great numbers in anticipation of sudden demand. Indeed the librarian is in the happy position of being able to stock up on copies of a popular book in great demand *after* the requests have been made and some use a rule of thumb of 'one extra copy for every five' (or whatever number is chosen) requests.

The advertising or publicity carried out by the library can be regarded as a desirable function of the service, but it is not essential to its success. A *good* library service *will* arrange special displays of books for loan on topical or special subjects and it *will* print lists of recent accessions and recommended titles and authors in various categories of fiction and non-fiction to help extend the readers' interests. Most public libraries have quite active informational activities. For example, the Sheffield City Library service prints a monthly bulletin called *Books of the Month* which not only draws attention to new titles in both fiction and non-fiction but also gives short bibliographies for special subjects. The April 1970 issue includes sections headed 'At Home and Abroad', 'Literature', 'Education', 'Railways', and 'Entertainment' and has a special bibliography of thirty references to Dylan Thomas. From time to time special bibliographies of about fifty to a hundred references are published; December 1969 had one on 'Language and Literature', March 1970 saw one on 'Sports and Pastimes', and after the death of Bertrand Russell there was one on his writings.

Camden Public Libraries regularly produce very attractively designed brochures and pamphlets as well as a bi-monthly magazine called the *Camden Journal* which is issued free. Special brochures for children's reading show good insight into the value of books in special situations. For example, two short brochures called *Smoothing the Path* give lists of books to reassure young children about to go into hospital and young children about to enter school for the first time. There are also special brochures for teen-age readers called *15 to 19* to help make the transition to fully adult reading. These very praiseworthy activities are not, however, usually regarded as a basic part of the library service and publicity and advertising often receive only small budgets. Undoubtedly a great deal more could be done by public libraries to try to attract more people to use the libraries and more thought could be given to attractive displays of books, but a library is not a shop and libraries do not work under the economic pressures which operate on booksellers.

The presence of books in the home can be considered from a number of viewpoints. It is generally accepted by educationalists that the child who comes from a home where there are books is more likely to be successful in his reading at school. The presence of books in the home is a manifestation of values which incorporate literacy and the acceptance of reading as a natural part of living. But reading, especially of books, is a private and solitary occupation and there are many homes with inadequate facilities for the separate activities of members of the household and there are households in which private and individual activities such as reading are still viewed askance and even regarded as anti-social. Yet the possession of books is a mark of social status and there are homes in which books are owned by all members of the family and personal libraries are built up from an early age. In between the extremes of anti-books and bibliophiles lie the many people who have a limited number of books and here we must distinguish between what might be called 'active' and 'dormant' books. Many people have a limited number of books in their home, but the collection of books may be years old and more decorative than functional. These are the collections that may have been gathered at college or university but ended when marriage and children resulted

in a shortage of money for luxuries such as books. There is
the story of the clergyman who claimed that he could tell
when his brother clergy stopped thinking by looking at
their bookshelves. Bookshelves of this kind usually manage
to have a dead look about them, and random observation
suggests that when bookshelves have glass doors on them
the books behind the glass are less often used than books on
open shelves. Bookshelves themselves are interesting
pieces of furniture, since they are specialised items and, in
natural wood, can be very beautiful and quite expensive.
Yet it is not easy to buy bookcases in Britain from ordinary
furniture shops. Office furnishers will sell them and high-
class furnishers may have several types to offer, but, in
general, the ordinary multiple store hire-purchase
furnisher will probably offer a glass-fronted china cabinet
as a bookcase. Unless one buys bookshelves from specialist
firms the simplest way to obtain them ready-made is in
whitewood, ready for painting or staining. Of course,
many people make their own, fit shelves in alcoves or put
rows of shelving on the modern style adjustable brackets.
But these forms all point to the fact that the ordinary set of
bookshelves is not an accepted article of British furniture.
So when the Booksellers Association of Great Britain put
their pamphlet 'Living with Books' in the May 1970 issue of
Homes and Gardens and emphasised how books could be
decorative aspects of the home beautiful they were aiming
at a group of readers who are likely to be receptive to the
ideas of homes with books and who are probably able to
accommodate them elegantly in sufficient space. Though
it must be recognised that the impact of the 'Living with
Books' insert was probably greatly decreased by inserts for

Time-Life on cooking and Dorma sheets and pillowcases being included in the one magazine. A similar plea to the working-class council house or flat tenant would be harder to design.

In general, then, it seems that books are seen regularly and normally by a limited section of the adult population. It is estimated that about a third of people do not use bookshops, about a third of people never use libraries, and about a third of people have virtually no books at home. Clearly then there are large numbers of people, especially in the working classes, who have very little visual contact at all with books. To people who like books this is a sad thing because not only are books intrinsically satisfying through their contents, but with modern dust-jackets and paperback covers they are decorative too. Books have many forms of appeal, intellectual, recreative, aesthetic and status conferring, and for them to have no place in people's lives results in quite substantial social deprivation.

Reading about Books
In this section we shall limit our discussion to the contact people have with books through reviews, news items and general advertising in the public press. It is now estimated that people aged 16 or over in this country see, on average, one daily morning newspaper and two Sunday newspapers. Annual readership surveys show that some mass-circulation papers are read by large proportions of the population and Table 1 gives some figures for the principal papers taken from the Joint Industry Committee for National Readership Surveys (JICNARS) National Readership Survey, July 1968–June 1969.

Table 1

Daily Papers	Circulation in 000s	% of population aged 16 and over reading the paper	Sunday Papers	Circulation in 000s	% of population aged 16 and over reading the paper
Daily Mirror	4,937	36.9	News of the World	6,179	39.5
Daily Express	3,759	26.5	People	5,441	38.9
Daily Mail	2,016	14.0	Sunday Mirror	5,012	34.5
Daily Telegraph	1,380	8.8	Sunday Express	4,221	26.5
Sun	980	8.2	Sunday Times	1,447	9.5
Daily Sketch	878	8.1	Observer	866	6.3
The Times	426	3.1	Sunday Mail	763	5.3
Guardian	290	2.2	Sunday Telegraph	750	5.2
Financial Times	168	1.8			

Note:—The *Daily Record* and *Sunday Post* are excluded because they are primarily Scottish papers.

As the table demonstrates, certain 'popular' papers have large circulations and are read by sizeable proportions of the population, whilst what are sometimes called 'quality' newspapers, such as *The Times*, the *Guardian* and the *Daily Telegraph*, are read by much smaller proportions of people. The smaller readership papers tend to give more space to books than do the mass-circulation papers, giving an inverse correlation between the popularity of the paper and the attention it gives to books.

This problem of books in the press was looked at in two ways. Firstly we had the good fortune to have a Sheffield library school student, Miss M. Scaife, carry out a study of one month's newspapers under our supervision. She analysed the amount of reviewing, advertising and news items on books so as to compare what happened in the various papers. Also I myself interviewed a number of literary editors of the general daily and Sunday newspapers with a predetermined set of questions to find out how the various papers dealt with reviewing. These two studies now provide the findings to illustrate how newspapers deal with books.

The analysis of the treatment of books in newspapers was carried out between 13 November and 10 December 1967 at the time when *Last Exit to Brooklyn* was the subject of criminal prosecution. This one book received more coverage than anything else in the world of books at the time and it was dealt with in a variety of ways by the press. The quality papers tended to report the court proceeding in a fairly matter-of-fact way, but for some popular newspapers the case was clearly another 'scandal' item, helped along by the appearance of well-known witnesses such as David Sheppard, referred to in one paper as 'the cricketing parson'. Apart from the *Last Exit* case no single book was a centre for any continued reporting. What clearly does happen in the news though is that books, and authors, make useful items for news articles or snippets in gossip columns. Treatment may vary from Peterborough's column in the *Daily Telegraph*, where literary gossip covers literary prizes in France and appointments in Britain to Chairs of English Literature across to William Hickey in the *Daily Express* or Henry Fielding in the *Sun*, where items may refer to copyright problems with *Ulysses* or interesting place names drawn from the new *Penguin Dictionary of Place Names*. In the general news coverage well-known authors often warrant more attention than their books, and details of their divorces, separations and the like are frequently reported upon. In the quality press the correspondence columns not infrequently have letters on books, especially when correspondents believe that they can correct inaccuracies contained in new books.

Of all the daily papers *The Times* generally has the broadest coverage of books in all ways, and the differences between the *Sunday Times*, *Observer* and *Sunday Telegraph* and the other Sunday papers are quite striking. Not only do the quality papers have regular review pages of appreciable size, they may also devote space to special sections on books. For instance the *Sunday Times* of 3 December 1967 had a special eight-page section on 'Books for Christmas'. The *Sunday Telegraph* of the same date had a section headed 'My Book of the Year' with contributors including Sir Donald Wolfit, Pamela Hansford Johnson and Beverley Nichols, whilst the *Sunday Times* of 20 November 1969 had a similar 'Critics Choice' with Jacquetta Hawkes and Hugh Trevor-Roper amongst the writers.

Publishers' advertising of books (apart from book clubs) is almost wholly restricted to the quality papers and it is noticeable that the regular advertisers are limited to a fairly small group of under a dozen well-known publishers. From time to time advertisements for erotic books appear in small advertisements and these too are restricted to the quality press. Advertising for book clubs does occur in popular papers, but as the costs of advertising are high in the mass-circulation papers it is not surprising to find them fairly restricted. A noticeable feature is the use of colour supplements for book club advertising and in these the use of colour enables the advertisers to make the books look much more attractive than can be done in simple black and white.

When we look at the actual reviewing of books in the newspapers the distinction between the quality and the popular papers becomes most marked. Books are dealt with as 'literature' in *The Times*, *Guardian* and *Daily Telegraph* and the *Sunday Times*, *Observer* and *Sunday Telegraph*. In addition the *Financial Times* has a genuine review page. No other papers can really be said to have any great breadth of coverage of books on a regular basis and their treatment tends to be journalistic rather than literary. In talking to literary editors it became clear that there are two quite distinct approaches. One group of literary editors is quite distinctly 'literary' in its approach and is concerned with arranging for books on a variety of subjects to be reviewed by experts of various types. The other group may only be concerned with picking out one or two books for any lengthy comment and that comment will be of a general nature, often geared to the topicality and news value of the book chosen. In the latter case the literary editors often do most of the reviewing themselves rather than have outsiders commissioned for the particular books, and one journalist referred to books in general as providing 'cheap copy'.

The survey and the interviews together found a surprising similarity in the books which were reviewed in all newspapers. Clearly the quality papers review *more* books and review them rather more expertly. But allowing for the smaller number of books dealt with in the popular papers it was surprising to see that their books were nearly always included in the bigger lists of the quality papers. *The Times* and the *Sunday Times* usually have a wider coverage than the other quality papers and the tabloid papers such as the *Daily Mirror* and *Daily Sketch*, along with their Sunday versions, have the smallest coverage. But practically all the papers had something to say about the diaries of Sir Henry 'Chips' Cannon and the letters of Groucho Marx, and the Cannon diaries were serialised in the *Sunday Telegraph*. These two books are useful examples of the type of 'personal' literature that frequently attracts either review or news attention. Yet, by contrast, the *Daily Mail*, which may be regarded as a middle-range daily paper, had reviews of a three-guinea book on Japanese flower arranging and an encyclopaedia of wine.

In my discussions with various literary editors it appeared that they were normally given a very free hand as to the way in which they dealt with reviewing. The amount of space available for the 'literary page(s)' was usually determined by general editorial policy and the literary editor could find himself squeezed for space by other sections of the paper although space given to publishers' advertising is generally regarded as outside the space allocated to reviewing. Once allocated his amount of space the literary editor then decides for himself how to apportion it to the various reviews. Quality papers often have well-known reviewers who write only for them and these 'contract' writers are usually given prominence in the review lay-out and have considerable freedom of choice in the books they choose to review. Other reviewers may be responsible for dealing with blocks of new fiction, detective stories, children's books or science fiction. In the popular newspapers it is much more common to find one book being given a lengthy review and a few others being dealt with very briefly so that they are 'mentioned' rather than reviewed. Of course, the quality papers devote more space altogether to books than do the popular press and readership figures indicate that the quality papers have a higher occupational status and better educated readership. The quality press reviews can thus be pitched at a higher level and one literary editor described his imaginary review reader as being 'at about the intellectual level of the bright sixth former or undergraduate.' It is then the literary editor's job to see that, the *level* of reviewing being determined, the *range* of books dealt with will be of interest. Here a significant point is how alike the various literary editors appear to be in their choices. In discussions it seemed that two processes operate in determining what gets on to the review pages. Firstly there is the process of discarding, which means getting rid of highly specialised books which may be either completely inappropriate to a general paper because of their particular specialisms or more suited to other specialised pages of the paper. In this way gardening, motoring, sport, financial and fashion pages have books passed to them which provide copy. In rather more important ways books of topical interest are used as a basis for feature articles on the main pages of the paper, and this can have an important effect on the main articles, especially of the Sunday quality papers, when political biographies are used for copy. Here the distinction between books as 'literature' and books as 'news' becomes blurred and it is probably a very useful thing for the world of books that this does happen since the 'news' pages may well be read by people who do not look very closely at the literary pages.

The second process is that of choosing from the books left after the preliminary selection and it was agreed that certain well-known fiction writers were always reviewed and though reviewers may feel that Mr X or Miss Y had written a rather poor novel this time no one was able to say if the subsequent sales were poor *because* of the reviews. Whilst publishers were eager to have their books reviewed it was generally accepted that no real pressure was exerted on literary editors, who themselves seemed to have a nice balance of good personal relations with publicity departments coupled with fairly shrewd assessments of how genuine their enthusiasms were.

Again, one is brought back to the sheer quantity of books that go on to the market. Whilst, clearly, 23,000 new titles a year do not all go to the general press, one literary editor did say that, in a busy week, he could receive up to 150 books. Many of these would be discarded on sight, a few would clearly stand out as books that people had been waiting for and which demanded review. But between the two extremes there would be many which could or could not be reviewed according to his judgment. Interestingly, the new fiction seemed to be the area where everyone wanted to make a discovery. Even though a first novel by an unknown author has relatively little chance of becoming a best seller, the literary world is always on the look out for the new writer and the literary editors clearly enjoy the opportunity to discover new talent. Often new novels are 'sieved' through several layers of reviewers of different levels of importance, and publishers' publicity departments can try to 'make' a new writer by intensive publicity and advertising. The search for the genuine new creative talent is an exciting one, and again points to the interest which attaches to the *person* as against the book. Outstanding though biography or literary criticism may be, the literary pages (and the literary prizes) tend to raise more excitement when they deal with people who write rather than what they write. This may explain the interest aroused by literary luncheons, authors' appearances, 'meet the writers' trips and the short lists for such prizes as the Booker Prize For Fiction. The writers rather than their books attract the attention of the general public through the media of the press, and, of course, as every fiction publisher will agree, it is *authors* who sell rather than books.

On the whole, therefore, it can be said that when people learn about books from what they read in the general press they are frequently learning to identify authors, and this may be done through both news and literary columns.

It has not been possible to look in any systematic fashion at magazines or specialist journals and their treatment of books, though useful studies could be carried out on these publications. A preliminary look at a complete collection of general periodicals, including all weekly and monthly publications from the *New Statesman* to *Red Letter*, indicated that apart from the obvious literary political journals such as the *New Statesman*, the *Spectator* and the *Listener* which have regular review sections but relatively small circulations, the popular magazines (and especially the popular women's magazines) with large circulations give very little space to books at all. Reviewing tends to be slight and superficial and usually restricted to books with clear relevance to the women's interests which are dealt with by the magazines themselves. Only the rather ardently feminist magazines such as *Nova* appear to attempt to intellectualise over books. In the magazines aimed specially at teenage readers one is, on the whole, in a world unaware of books apart from a note on the occasional light-weight paperback, although serialisation of romantic novels is an important way for novelists to become known to magazine readers.

Specialist journals may be taken to cover all interests from camping to crystallography. The brief study of journals did not include these categories, but from a cursory look it is clear that many 'hobbies' magazines or such similar periodicals are not very adept at dealing with book reviews. Anyone who has ever reviewed books knows how difficult it is to 'review' a book in very few words, and many periodicals may not wish to give more than 200 words at most to a book review. As a result, reviewing in the commercially produced 'hobbies' and 'interest' journals is often of low quality, frequently précis rather than review, and tucked away in an obscure part of the periodical. The relatively low apparent status of these contributions is an interesting reflection on the way that the journals do not lead the readers on to books. By contrast, reviewing in academic specialist journals is a very serious matter indeed and in the advanced sciences where information is in a state of flood review journals can be of the very greatest importance.

Hearing about Books

As has already been said, it would be very difficult to

discover how much the general population actually hears about books. Conventional survey methods would not be suitable as recall of such talk would be very difficult for people to carry out. The mind turns to such advanced techniques as micro tape-recorders carried about all day with every conversation subsequently analysed, a tedious business and largely unprofitable. What is clear from discussions with people in the world of publishing and bookselling is that *they* believe that there are people who do 'talk books' a great deal. Publishers have spoken of the sales of books, especially in the serious non-fiction and fiction categories, which seem to have been influenced by becoming 'known' through talk. A good deal of this talk is believed to occur in the Greater London area rather than the provinces, and it should be noted that, since the hard-back copy of a first novel by an unknown author could sell as few as 500 copies to private bookshop buyers in this country, it does not need a very great amount of interest in the book to raise purchases to a few thousands, which could put the book in the category of a 'good' seller, though clearly not a 'best' seller. No one knows how the grapevine of book talk works, but (rather in the way that serious theatre audiences appear to operate) 'the word gets around' that a new book, like a new theatre production, is worthy of attention. Since books in the general categories tend to be reviewed very quickly after publication (having been supplied by publishers weeks before so as to ensure review on publication) this talk can be a result of reading about books, but it is something more than this. People who have a deep and genuine interest in books as such are clearly a minority in the population, but they tend to be an articulate (even at times garrulous) minority, and in the literary world there is a certain status to be achieved by being 'in' on the latest publications, hence the importance of the review pages and the literary gossip columns as indications of the latest trends. But by contrast the world outside books can be a cold and chilly place for the book reader. As an experiment, we would recommend to the literary people that they attend a cocktail party or such similar occasion where the middle-class attenders are from industries or trades that have nothing specifically to do with books. To attempt to introduce chat about the latest novels or historical biographies in these groups can be an unrewarding experience. It is thus necessary to be aware that it does not seem that the general public, even the middle-class public, lives in a world in which books are a common focus of general conversation.

When one turns to the spoken word on radio or television it becomes clear that the expected audience is the band of the converted. In broadcasting, books are dealt with in only a very small minority of programmes. News items rarely deal with books as such, although court cases dealing with obscenity or civil damages for libel frequently receive mentions. The deaths of well-known writers are also usually reported on the sound news, though not always on television. 'Magazine' programmes do, from time to time, deal with books which attract attention and there seems to be a slight increase in this trend. But, in general, it can be appreciated that books as such do not make very good television material, and television programmes, especially news and magazine programmes, show a clear tendency to exploit the medium of the moving picture wherever possible, so serious books and unspectacular authors do not rate high as television interest catchers.

On the conventional radio, however, the spoken word is the medium and so 'talking about books' can become a minority form of programme. Under the new system of broadcasting in the seventies there has been a change from the half-hour per week of book reviewing called 'The World of Books' to a three-quarters of an hour programme with the unattractive title 'Now Read on . . .' and the long-running 'A Book at Bedtime' has been extended from thirteen to fifteen minutes. Occasionally general programmes such as 'The Arts This Week' also deal with books. But on the whole the sound radio gives relatively little attention to books as books from a review point of view. Books, in abridged form, are read on 'Story Time' for half an hour daily at 4.30 p.m., in 'A Book at Bedtime' daily for fifteen minutes at 11 p.m., and on 'Woman's Hour' near the end of the 2 to 3 p.m. programme. Clearly books read on the radio must be abridged, since it is estimated that a 100,000 word novel would take twenty hours to read in its entirety. The abridged versions are carefully edited and the range of books chosen for these readings is very catholic. It is said that the producer of 'A Book at Bedtime' reads 300 books a year to help choose the right ones for broadcasting.

But whilst some people may enjoy having abridged versions of books read to them the very timing of the programmes must of necessity exclude many potential listeners. Much more attention is drawn to books by dramatised presentations, and particularly effective is dramatisation for television. The BBC television presentation of *The Forsyte Saga* was one of their greatest successes in television drama and led to tremendous sales of the various books by Galsworthy which made up the saga. The use of photographs of the television actors on the paperback covers helped identify the books with the television series and, for a time, the country seemed to have a minor epidemic of Soames mania. Yet, as has been pointed out by literary critics, the Forsyte books are by no means the greatest literature this country has ever produced, and in many ways the television series was far more interesting than the books. Thus whilst not ignoring the *sales* of the Forsyte books which television undoubtedly stimulated, it would seem wise to wonder how many of these books still remain unread or unfinished by people who found the written word less stimulating than the television adaptation.

The same type of problem arises when considering the stimulus that a film version of a book may give. It is clear that the James Bond films and the James Bond books tend to promote interest in each other. Powerful light fiction consumption can be promoted by tying in with films and publishers' publicity departments give great attention to utilising the enormous publicity potential of films, especially when famous actors appear in them. A good example is the paperback edition of Alistair Maclean's *Where Eagles Dare*, the cover of which is dominated by a photograph of Richard Burton and carries a small reminder 'Now a stunning Winkast film – Presented by M.G.M.' On the back cover there is a further photograph of Burton with a blonde who is wearing a very low-cut blouse. Just in case the reader does not notice that the man in the photograph is Richard Burton the top of the back cover declares ' "The best adventure story I have ever read", Richard Burton'. The tie-in between film or television production and books is an important part of publicity for books, although this tends to occur much more in the light-fiction section than any other. Clearly the visual presentation in the cinema or on television draws people's attention to the books, and any railway station paperback display demonstrates the considerable numbers of links between the two media. What cannot be guaranteed is that viewers will be satisfied by the written form of what they have enjoyed seeing and hearing. Both the 1927 and the 1959 film versions of *Ben Hur* have been highly placed amongst the cinema's most popular films and have been great money-makers. The book from which the films have been made is one which many readers today would probably find very long-winded and hard to get through. Philip Purser, the television critic of the *Sunday Telegraph*, wrote on the serialisation of books that 'any television adaptation is a ruthless and rather crude abridgment of the original. Perhaps half the famous story has had to go, two-thirds of the detail and three-quarters of the subtlety'. Yet he admitted that some very unexpected candidates had 'hooked' him for series on BBC2 and he expressed surprise at being interested by the television versions of 'a dreary old Zola, and Stella Gibbons' heavy-handed romp, and now Arnold Bennett's *Imperial Palace*.' The problem is therefore one of long and short-term satisfactions. It would be hard to deny the value of the attention drawn to books by television or cinema adaptations, and in the more ephemeral world of light romances and thrillers the two media support each other: it is far more problematical whether the television and cinema versions of more serious books, and especially dated 'classics', do really have any long-term effect upon people's interests in books and reading. The New English Version of the Bible created more interest in the Bible than did the film of this name, which a film critic announced was clearly *not* the film of the book.

Receiving Information about Books

As has already been pointed out, advertising of books is a difficult activity since many books of a specialised type are not intended for general readerships and a sale of 3,000 over a period of two or three years may be quite acceptable. When a specialist book may only warrant a total advertising budget of well under £200 there is not a great deal that can be done to promote it in 'broadcast' fashion. It is therefore desirable to limit promotion of specialist books to people who are likely to be interested in them. This can be done to some extent by advertising in, and sending review copies to, appropriate journals but this cannot ensure that everyone who may be interested will actually see the advertisements or reviews. The more direct method is by mailing advertisements direct to likely book purchasers. This raises problems of actually obtaining samples of the appropriate people since lists of people may not be obtained very easily. Even if published lists are available, as for medical practitioners, clergy or university teachers, the particular interests of these people may not be known and it could be quite an expensive matter for publishers to mail all their advertising in say, chemistry, to every member of a university chemistry department.

Some publishers do work on this relatively wide-net system and a great deal of their advertising is bound to be wasted, yet the drawing of people's attention to books outside their particular specialisms might induce them to obtain a copy of a book through a library if not by purchase. No one can hope to know. Another way of going about the task has been demonstrated by the organisation known as the University Mailing Service which acts as a coordinating distributor of personal advertising for any publishers who wish to subscribe to their association. In this scheme the UMS attempts to discover the interests of academics by means of a detailed questionnaire in which the recipient ticks his teaching, research and peripheral interests within certain fields of study and then the UMS sends advertising literature of a more restricted nature to the recipient from the subscribing publisher. This scheme has the advantage of mailing several publishers' advertisements together at regular intervals and thus economising on postage and literature. It is also felt that, in these days when academics are inundated by advertising, some limitation of post is to the good so as not to build up resistance to the familiar second-class postage brown envelopes.

The problem is a difficult one and there are interesting differences of viewpoint manifested in the approaches used in direct advertising. Some publishers clearly like to use a somewhat fulsome approach, even to the point of a fac-simile letter stressing the value of their new book. Others prefer the softer sell approach of the Publishers' Information Cards Service which are very clear and neat in setting out purely informative details of books on $5'' \times 3''$ cards which can easily be indexed by the recipients. The 'PICS' system works on a basic assumption that relevance is the factor that will interest the specialist rather than fulsome self-commendatory phrases. Even more recently a rather similar system of informational cards from several publishers sent to schools has been initiated by a company called 'Infopacks' who mail to various *types* of teachers in schools (though not to named individuals). The Infopack cards all have detachable reply-paid request cards so that recipients can send back for inspection copies of books that interest them. Offers of copies to view, which can be retained if the book is subsequently recommended to a reasonable sized class of students, is a fairly common ploy used by individual academic publishers hoping to have textbooks 'adopted' in the American fashion. With the increasing competition in the textbook market in the rapidly growing social sciences, this system is becoming used much more by British publishers.

As yet no systematic research has been published, or is known to have been carried out, on the results of direct advertising, though it is claimed by the UMS organisation that sales of their subscribing publishers' books have risen appreciably – though whether they have risen more than those of non-member publishers who are saying nothing cannot be known. Since publishers *are* in competition with each other they are understandably disinclined to tell their competitors too much about their most successful gambits, or their unsuccessful ones. What is clearly needed in the area of general research is a long-term study of the whole way in which academic books are bought, borrowed and lent by students, staff, libraries and everyone else connected with books in education. This would be a limited study at the school level where books are provided for students, but in higher education, and especially in universities where breadth of reading is encouraged and library holdings may be vast, there is a need for systematic studies of how people, staff and students alike, come to know about books, decide to borrow or buy books and how they view books in general as tools in the educational process. Such a study would have tremendous value to everyone, staff, student, bookseller and publisher alike, and with the potential increase in student numbers in the 1970s and 80s the desirability of such a study becomes increasingly clearer. What few studies have been carried out on how students learn about books have been very empirical in their approach and largely made by librarians. What is needed is a much wider viewpoint to take in the whole idea of 'book culture' in higher education.

For the ordinary reader, not a known specialist in any particular field of study, direct advertising is hardly worth contemplating because of the small returns for outlay. There are instances, from time to time, of advertising matter about books on certain aspects of sex going through the post to highly unsuitable people such as clergy or babes in arms. One does wonder if some of these ploys may be intended as attempts to gain publicity in the press as much as for the advertising value itself. For a publisher a book to be denounced by an irate clergyman or MP can be useful publicity in certain spheres of activity.

Conclusions

Much of this chapter has been descriptive rather than

quantitative since so little data exist about the means by which people learn about books. What is clear, however, is that a great deal of information of all kinds is restricted largely to those people who, in general, are already within book culture. We would not go so far as to suggest that Disraeli's two worlds still exist, but the analysis of the press indicates that newspapers and magazines tend to write for two sorts of people, and that there is relatively little 'evangelism' for books in the popular press.

The same can be said of the media of radio and television, in which books receive little attention and where attention is given it tends to be of a rather distinctly 'literary' type.

If the third of the population who may be considered to be completely out of touch with books are to be made aware of books, and if the half of the population who may be generally said to be barely in touch with books are to be reached, it is clear that the evangelistic excursions must be based upon known interests where books may have a natural place. The *Homes and Gardens* approach was quite unashamedly a snob appeal approach stressing the decorative as well as literary functions of books to a very high-class magazine readership. Such people have money and space for books and they can be encouraged to buy more books. At the other end of the social scale people have less space and less money, but they may well have very practical interests for which books can be very helpful if they are more aware of what exists. Here the advertising and publicity available through quite high circulation hobbies and practical interest magazines could be developed more systematically, and whilst it would not be acceptable for publishers' publicity departments to offer ready-written reviews they could probably help more with information about the books and gentle pressure to extend and improve review pages.

The public libraries, too, without taking a commercial view, could not be displeased if they were to extend even further the numbers of people who use their services. There is a danger of thinking that because public libraries are *available* to everyone that they are actually *used* by everyone and this is not so. Clearly there are large numbers of people, young and old, who do not use their libraries, where the use of books is offered as a public service borne by public funds. The function of the library service is not easy to fulfil, since it has a duty to provide for both educational and recreational interests, but if recreational interests were held to be equal with educational ones, then the image of the public library could change and the slightly fusty or forbidding ideas that non-users may have of their libraries could be dispelled. The old saying about being able to lead a horse to water but not being able to make it drink may be true, but if the horse never ever gets near to water at all it will stay thirsty until it dies.

Chapter 2

Books as Gifts

Introduction

Late in 1967 Smythsons of Bond Street, a very high-class stationery shop, had a window display which showed a small number of expensive books with a placard alongside them which advertised 'Books for Beautiful Gifts'. These carefully chosen beautiful and expensive books were obtainable from the 'Book Boutique'. Not everyone would consider this a typical example of books as gifts and, indeed, it is chosen to show how at one extreme books may be offered for sale as objects of beauty rather than as forms of communication. The book as a gift is an interesting phenomenon, since it is acknowledged that ownership of books confers status, and, therefore, to give books is also a status-conferring action. Booksellers will know that a sizeable proportion of their trade, especially before Christmas, depends on the gift market. Publishers deliberately time the publication of certain books so as to catch the Christmas market and the buying of children's 'annuals' (a large and important book market which it seems rather *infra dig.* to discuss in public) may well be the one occasion in the year when some people actually do buy a 'book'. Very little of a systematic nature is known about books as gifts. The ERC survey of 1965 found that 30 per cent of the population claimed to have bought a book as a gift the previous Christmas. Gift buying was particularly strong amongst the upper classes (the AB group) amongst whom two-thirds had given a book compared with 59 per cent of the lower middle class (C_1) and only 16 per cent of the working class (C_2DE). The popularity of book buying is therefore more than four times as great amongst the upper classes as the working class. But it must also be noted that the working class is approximately four times as big as the upper classes and so if the class distribution of the actual buyers of books as gifts is calculated it is seen that, roughly speaking, these buyers were one-third upper class, one-third lower middle class, and one-third working class.

Table 2

Bought a Book as a Gift last Christmas

Social class	Bought book gift	Distribution of sample	Distribution of gift buyers
Upper (AB) .	67	14	31
Lower Middle (C_1)	59	18	34
Working (C_2DE)	16	68	35
All sample	30	100	100

A similar result, though not quite as marked, comes from the question which asked people if they had received a book as a gift during the past year. Here just over half the upper class and the lower middle class had, compared with only 17 per cent of the working class. But when the data were reworked and the class distribution of all the recipients was calculated, the table then showed that the largest proportion of recipients was actually the working class (41%) with the lower middle class second (34%) and the upper class last (26%).

Table 3

Received a Book as a Gift in Past Year

Social Class	Received book as gift	Distribution of sample	Distribution of recipients
Upper (AB) .	52	14	26
Lower Middle (C₁)	54	18	34
Working (C₂DE)	17	68	41
All sample	28	100	100

Whilst sample surveys are always open to error in the data which they collect it should be noted that the ERC survey is one of the very few general book surveys based on a national sample (2,300 people). But the use of the word 'book' raises problems in research such as this. Not only must it include everything from the cheapest paperback to the most expensive art book, it must also cover cookery books, car manuals, road guides, even textbooks – in fact a whole host of books which fall outside 'literature' and which may well be purchased from retail outlets other than conventional bookshops. The complete field of books as gifts therefore includes a very wide range of books and only highly detailed research, necessitating very carefully chosen samples and considerable research resources, could hope to produce the full picture of this interesting aspect of book culture.

In continuance of the policy of pilot studies a survey was made of recipients of Christmas books and gift buying was studied by looking at 'book tokens' as a form of gift substitute. The results of these surveys now follow.

Books as Christmas Gifts

The period just before Christmas is a very important one for the book trade and particularly affects the over-the-counter sales in general bookshops. Market research studies suggest that many people who buy books as Christmas gifts are not regular book buyers and booksellers have confirmed this to us from their own experiences.

Clearly the best way to study Christmas book buying would be by a survey of those people who have given and received books for Christmas, but this raises great practical problems. A survey of the general population is not only expensive and time-consuming, but also is likely only occasionally to turn up the giver or recipient. A survey of people buying books carried out inside or on the doorstep of a busy bookshop just before Christmas would not only hinder the bookselling but could also annoy busy shoppers. So it was decided to try to obtain information after Christmas from the recipients of books as Christmas presents so as to avoid the pre-Christmas problem and, it was hoped, to gain some insights into the acceptability of the books received. Valid sampling could not be expected for this study since no sample frame existed to draw from, so it was decided to try to contact people who had received books or book tokens for Christmas through local newspapers and radio. The survey was reported as a news item in feature columns of the *Yorkshire Post* and *Sheffield Star* (evening paper) and a letter was printed in the ordinary correspondence column by the *Sheffield Telegraph* (morning paper). The attempt to use Radio Sheffield was not successful since the interview ran out of time just before the six o'clock news and the Radio Sheffield interviewer did not give listeners the address for contact. In the end letters asking for copies of the questionnaire were received from seventy-four people, some of whom said they would distribute copies to friends whom they knew had received books. Letters received varied in style and indicated different types of personality amongst the writers. One said, 'If Dixon Lane [the columnist in the *Sheffield Star*] was not joking and you really do want to know, I had a book for Christmas', whilst a more formal note read 'Miss X has read your article in the *Yorkshire Post* and is willing to receive your questionnaire with a view to completing and returning it to you.' Other writers demonstrated a desire to help because the survey was about books and this was well illustrated by the lady who wrote, 'Whilst being strongly "agin" filling in forms etc., this is one case when I shall be only too pleased to assist you in your worthwhile work by completing your questionnaire to the best of my limited ability.' In general it was clear from the initial letters that the people who wrote to us were predominantly middle-aged to elderly and were, on the whole, people who had a genuine feeling for books. If the ERC findings are correct in suggesting that more young than old people give and receive books as presents then our self-selected sample is *not* typical of *all* book givers and receivers, but is rather an example of books as gifts amongst the older age groups.

The Respondents

A minimum of six copies of the questionnaire were sent in reply to each letter and people were asked to fill in one for each book or book token. Replies were received from 112 people giving details of 165 books and 47 book tokens. Replies from three people were unanalysable, reducing the people concerned to 109, and of these 72 were women and 37 men. Taken together, 8 per cent were under 18, 25 per cent were between 18 and 34, 27 per cent were between 35 and 54, and 38 per cent were 55 or over, with 31 per cent actually in the 55–64 age group. Age differences between the sexes were not great, though there were rather more men of 45–54 and rather more women of 35–44. There were practically no manual workers, though 50 per cent of respondents were in the category C_1, which includes lower management, semi-professions, technicians and office workers; 26 per cent were in category B, which covers middle management and lesser professions, and only 8 per cent were in category A (the higher executive, managerial and professional grades). Seven per cent could only be classified as housewives and 4 per cent gave no details, leaving 6 per cent in the C_2 category (supervisory and skilled manual workers). This breakdown shows a solid middle-class group of respondents, though the weight is towards the lower rather than the upper middle class. It is interesting to note at this point that the class structure is similar to that found in the survey of book token purchases made in Manchester and London, even though the age distributions are very different.

With such a high general age there were not many respondents with children at home – only 24 out of 109 had, and of these 7 had children over the age of 16 at home.

The educational background of respondents was also high. Twenty-nine per cent had finished their education at grammar schools, 14 per cent at public or private schools, 15 per cent at colleges of further education (e.g., art, secretarial, technical) and 21 per cent had been to university. The higher age groups represented by our respondents and traditional sex differences in higher education were reflected by greater proportions of men who had been to university or public school and more women who had been to secretarial or similar colleges. One woman lamented, 'I was educated at home and I have been catching up ever since.'

Tastes in Reading

All the respondents were asked about their tastes in reading and the replies were then categorised into a dozen types. Biography was the most popular type of book with both men and women, half of all respondents mentioning this category, though a higher proportion of women (58%) than men (35%) mentioned it. General novels were second in overall popularity (38% mention) though they were equal with thrillers and mystery stories for men. In overall choice travel tied for third place with thrillers and mystery (each 29% mention), but travel books were mentioned more frequently by women than men. Reference works came next at fifth[1] place (20% overall) and were fifth for men as against equal sixth for women. Poetry, drama and belles-lettres were equal sixth overall, tying at 21 per cent mentions with historical novels, but both of these categories were better placed with women than men, the latter showing more interest in hobbies and what could be classified as statements meaning 'a wide range of tastes'. The interesting point about this analysis was that whilst

[1] As there was a tie for *third* place, the next place is counted as fifth.

the actual *numbers* of respondents showed women tending to mention more categories of books than the men, the general rank order of preference showed a similarity between the sexes in the leading favoured categories.

Table 4
Tastes in Books: First Five Choices

	Men			Women	
Order	Type of Book	% mention	Order	Type of Book	% mention
1	Biography	35	1	Biography	58
2	General novels	27	2	General novels	43
2	Thrillers/mystery	27	3	Travel	33
4	Travel	22	4	Thrillers/mystery	31
5	Reference works	16	5	Historical novels	24

There were numerous written-in comments to this question, many of which were most interesting. A teacher (aged 35–44) said 'I hate travel and autobiography' whilst a wool merchant (aged 55–64) wrote 'I have catholic tastes ruling out space fiction and romance.' For some people reading was clearly a serious matter. An unmarried secretary (aged 45–54) said 'During the last two years I have concentrated on books by Henry James and Virginia Woolf, also books I feel I should read, such as *Honest to God*. I have little interest in the post-war modern novel despite a course at the local technical college.' Another unmarried woman, a teacher (aged 25–34), said she liked 'good novels, especially *solid* ones, e.g., Russian.' Another woman teacher, retired, said she liked 'modern novels where the characterisation is good.'

Other respondents stressed more the importance of books as sources of information. A woman (aged 55–64) who described herself as a company director said she liked 'history, biography, travel, anything informative; never novels.' And the young (aged 18–24) wife of a quantity surveyor said she preferred 'informative books on a hobby or sport'.

As the respondents had shown interest in books as gifts to themselves they were asked whether or not they gave books as gifts to other people. Only 8 per cent gave an unqualified 'no' whilst 43 per cent gave an unqualified 'yes'. A further 12 per cent said 'occasionally', 12 per cent restricted their book gifts to children, and 16 per cent said they gave only to particular people whose tastes were known. The importance of the 'rightness' of a book as a gift was commented on in a number of ways. A woman university lecturer (aged 45–54) said she gave a book 'sometimes, if I am quite sure that I am giving the right book to the right person.' The wife of a university lecturer showed how giving books was easier when the donor has friends with a common interest in books. She wrote, 'We have many friends who regard buying books for themselves as a luxury, but they like to have them. I gave 19 books last Christmas, including seven to children.' She then added an interesting footnote, 'Having worked at one time for a publisher at a pittance, I feel the book trade needs all the support it can get.'

Book tokens were especially noted by two respondents for their convenience as gift substitutes. A woman civil servant (aged 25–34) said that she usually gave book tokens because she found it difficult to buy a suitable book and if she did find what she thought was suitable 'invariably I buy it and keep it myself.' The wife of a company director made a more practical point when she wrote, 'I usually give book tokens rather than risk giving a book someone doesn't want and also to save postage.'

Books Received at Christmas

The number of books received by respondents varied between one and six, but nearly two-thirds received one book and about a fifth two books. It was possible to analyse the details of 165 books in all. General reference works were most popular, followed by biography, then travel and general novels tying, with natural history close behind. Art and 'coffee table' books were next, with poetry and drama following. A comparison of the types of books which respondents had said they enjoyed most with the types of books which they actually received shows a rank order as follows:

Table 5

Books Preferred compared with Books Received:
Men and Women Together

	Preferred		Received
1	Biography	1	Reference works
2	General novels	2	Biography
= 3	Travel	= 3	Travel
= 3	Thrillers/ mystery	= 3	General novels
5	Reference works	5	Natural history

It may be seen from these comparisons that, in general, fiction comes out higher in the 'preferred' list than in the 'received', and that what might be considered 'safer' and less personal types of books predominate in the higher ranking 'received' categories. Historical novels and thriller/mystery stories come very low in the 'received' list and it may therefore be inferred that safety is an important factor in choosing books as gifts and probably many givers of books look for books which are likely to be *generally* acceptable rather than books which *particularly* suit the recipient's tastes. It had been expected that what are sometimes called 'coffee table' books might have loomed larger in the gifts received but in analysis of the books these only came sixth on the list. It is also noticeable that in the first five categories of books received only one is fiction, and that the more serious general fiction. Again this seems to indicate a somewhat serious approach to book choice, and it could be hypothesised that the givers of books may see the books they choose as reflecting on themselves and that there is a tendency to derive status from the choice of books. As a result of this status seeking the books chosen tend to have an element of seriousness about them which is reflected by the large element of non-fiction.

All recipients were asked to indicate whether the books they received were in hardback or paperback form and, rather surprisingly, almost a third of them were paperback copies. This goes rather against the idea of the status-conferring nature of book giving, but can be interpreted as an acceptance today of paperbacks as 'real' books and also, of course, the current price of many paperbacks hardly accords with the old idea of them as 'cheap editions'. The books themselves were given by a wide variety of people, but nearly two-thirds of the donors were relatives and the remainder were friends. Almost half of the gifts were exchanged within the basic family unit, between spouses, between parents and children, and (to a lesser degree) between brothers and sisters. The importance of the family as a unit for the exchange of gift books is highlighted by the fact that just over a third of the recipients had actually asked for a specific book, although it must also be recorded that over 60 per cent of recipients received 'surprise' book gifts. This did not mean, however, that the books themselves which were received were completely unknown; the recipients reported that 26 per cent of the books received had actually been read before, 46 per cent were known or had been heard of, and only the remaining 28 per cent were books that the recipient had not heard of previously.

Reactions to the Books Received

To receive a book as a gift may be pleasant, but having the book is no guarantee that the recipient will read it and one suspects that there must be many unread books on domestic bookshelves. The questionnaires for this survey mostly went out in January and replies came back well into March. To try to get some reaction to the books all respondents were asked if they had read their books, or in appropriate cases had used them for reference. Nearly 80 per cent of recipients claimed they had read or referred to their books, and another 15 per cent said they were reading them at the present time. Only about 5 per cent had not used them at all. It is, of course, possible that there was bias in these answers, since people may well not want to admit that they have not looked at the books they received.

To try to some extent to overcome this people were asked to comment on the books in any way they wished. Replies varied from the brief 'very interesting' to lengthy critiques of subject matter, style and even print and format. Many comments showed knowledge of the work of particular authors. A chartered secretary (aged 55–64) commented on Agatha Christie's *Endless Night*, 'Rather different from the author's previous books. A book you can't put down until you get to the end.' Another person said that a book was 'not one of Hammond Innes's best.' Several people commented on Mary Stewart's *The Gabriel Hounds* and showed that they had been awaiting her latest book.

Other comments on a variety of books showed that the readers were able to evaluate their gifts at a reasonable level of criticism, whilst still indicating their enjoyment. A retired auctioneer said of Harold Macmillan's *The Blast of War*, 'An excellent detailed account of the day-to-day life of a busy minister during the war years. Written in impeccable English.' A village postmistress (aged 45–54) said of Sir Arthur Bryant's *The Age of Chivalry*, 'I feel that history really comes to life in this book. All Sir Arthur Bryant's books do this and make me more optimistic about the present day.' A headmistress praised Josephine Tey's *The Daughter of Time* as 'Magnificent. I wish there were more like this to use as a basis for history teaching. I couldn't put it down.' A schoolgirl was quite overcome by Tolkien's *The Lord of the Rings*, 'The best book I have ever read. A wonderful, magnificent book.' A journalist had asked for a P. G. Wodehouse book and commented, 'I was chuckling over Wodehouse forty or more years ago and I am glad to find his books still amuse me immensely.'

More practical books were evaluated in perceptive ways. A book on Indian recipes received this comment from a housewife, 'Good recipes. No index – terrible omission in a reference book, I feel. Poor quality paper and I think cookery books should have "wipe clean" finish and cover.' A housewife (aged 55–64), formerly a teacher, commented on the *A.A. Book of the Road*, 'Good value, print clear, paper of good quality, maps conveniently arranged and in 'clean' colours. Useful articles, well illustrated. Long narrow shape at first unattractive, but probably convenient in the car.'

Reference works often appeared to have an attraction in themselves beyond merely supplying a particular piece of information for a specific problem. A nursing sister said of Mrs Beeton's *Household Management*, 'A mine of information. I begin looking for something specific and then usually end up reading huge chunks of it. All most interesting.' And a housewife (aged 55–64), who was once a director's secretary said of *The Teach Yourself Concise Encyclopedia of General Knowledge*, 'It whets the appetite for information. I pick it up to gather information for a problem and I am still reading it two hours later, dipping here and there.' More specifically a housewife (aged 45–54) noted how a particular reference book was helping to extend and deepen her knowledge in a special field of interest. Writing on *A Field Guide to the Birds of Britain and Europe* she commented, 'I refer to this book regularly. I think it absolutely marvellous: I am gradually learning to identify birds further afield than my garden. I only wish all the illustrations were in colour.'

Other recipients of books made comments which showed that they had been intellectually stimulated by books in a fairly wide range of categories. For some, new insights into personal and social problems had been gained through the books. A housewife (aged 55–64) commented on the South African situation as depicted in Alan Paton's *Cry the Beloved Country*, 'I have read this book twice and can see both sides of the question. First my sympathies are with one side and then the other, but I shouldn't care to have any part in solving it.' A clergyman (over 65 years of age), said that Leslie Weatherhead's *The Christian Agnostic* was 'Very challenging and stimulating. Makes me re-think my position re Christian beliefs.' Another clergyman (aged 25–34) said of Simon Masters' novel *A Door Closing*, 'This is an interesting novel by a very young author on the hopelessness of the teenage scene. It gives many insights into the situation which are very clearly expressed.'

Other books of a lighter type were appreciated or commented on at the appropriate level. A lady of 85 said that a book by Antonia Ridge was 'A very pleasant humorous refreshing story – very slight but enjoyable.' A housewife (aged 45–54) said that a collection of items from the radio programme 'Home this Afternoon' was 'very entertaining for short-term reading.' Another housewife described a book about children as 'Rubbish, but sweet rubbish.'

Adverse comments were usually brief and used such terms as 'boring', 'not up to much' and 'not as good as I expected'. One interesting comment came from a recipient who had been in hospital. She wrote 'The book was a surprise which arrived whilst I was in hospital, but it is far too heavy (in weight) to read in bed, a point often overlooked when books are bought as gifts for invalids.'

In general, however, the reaction to the gift books was favourable and about two-thirds of the books received fairly unqualified praise. It may therefore be concluded from this exploratory survey that books as gifts are, on the whole, successful choices. The surveyed sample is a rather special one, as it is heavily weighted with older middle-class people, but clearly this group must be an important part of the gift-book market. The choice of appropriate books seems to be a little on the conservative side, but the study seems to indicate that there are types of books (especially in non-fiction) which make reasonably successful gifts and the recipients seem, on the whole, to be satisfied with what they are given. Undoubtedly there is a status element in both giving and receiving books as Christmas presents, but the reactions of the recipients indicate that, status conferring though books may be in themselves, the contents are important and can give pleasure, knowledge and new insights. Books as gifts do, therefore, extend the personality of the recipient and may claim greater cultural value than silver-plated after-dinner mint holders or leather-bound bottle holders.

Book Tokens as Gift Substitutes

As the survey of books as Christmas gifts showed, it is not always easy to fit the particular book to the particular person and some people hedge on this by choosing books of a particular type which they hope will be generally acceptable. Other people go further than this and instead of giving a book at all they give a 'book token', which is a card to which is affixed a stamp for a chosen amount of money. The purchaser pays 4d. for the card plus the amount shown on the stamp and the recipient can then exchange the token at practically any bookshop or bookstall in the country for books to the value of the token. The book token system has the advantage of giving the recipient a completely free choice of books and, of course, it is much more cheaply sent through the post than is a book, especially in recent times when book post is expensive and unreliable. Against this some people seem to feel that giving a book token (or a record token or a Boots token) is rather a sign of desperation and an admission of being unable to find an appropriate personal gift. There is also the point that a book token is a money-substitute as well as a book-substitute and some people do not like giving sums of money as presents. Nevertheless the book token scheme (which is run by a limited company under the auspices of the Booksellers Association) is very popular and successful and practically all major outlets for the sale of books participate in it.

It was decided that, as part of the study of books as gifts, it would be helpful to try to find out something about the people who bought book tokens and also something about the ways in which they were spent. The book tokens purchase survey was carried out just before Christmas 1968 and was, as far as is known, the first survey ever made of book token purchasers.[1] The plan was to have paid students working in bookshops for about ten

[1] Since this initial survey Book Tokens Ltd. have commissioned a large-scale market research survey.

days before Christmas and for one student to be wholly responsible for the sale of tokens in that shop. In this way the bookseller would be relieved of this particular task for the survey period and the student would be able to ask each purchaser a small number of questions after each sale had been made. It would have been better to have had several students in various parts of the country and in different types and sizes of shops but financial resources and the cooperation offered limited the study to two shops in the end. Fortunately both were large and important shops, one in central London (Claude Gill of Oxford Street) and one in central Manchester (Sherratt & Hughes). We were most fortunate in the cooperation given to us by the management of these shops and in both places the survey was most successful.

The survey began on Monday, 16 December and went through until the shops closed on Tuesday, 24 December. The two students employed sold all the book tokens for their shops during this period and as well as noting the types of card and the values of the tokens they also asked the purchaser at each transaction:

1. For whom was the token being bought?
2. Was the token being given instead of an actual *book* or was it just an alternative form of general *gift*?
3. Had the purchaser ever bought a book token before?
4. How many tokens was he/she buying this Christmas?
5. Had he/she seen any advertising recently for book tokens? (There had been a campaign including television commercials in the north-west.)
6. What were the purchaser's sex, age and occupation (or husband's occupation for housewives).

Answers to these questions were recorded on simple standard forms, and the 'mini-interviews' took about two minutes each. In all 940 transactions were recorded, 326 in London and 614 in Manchester. Results were put on to punch cards and analysed mechanically. The results which follow are given separately for London and Manchester.

The Cards Bought

The range of cards offered by the two shops was not the same, since any bookseller may choose what cards to stock, and only 10 cards were offered at Claude Gill as compared to 18 at Sherratt & Hughes. For this reason no strict comparison between London and Manchester is possible, but what did stand out was the popularity of a very modern rather 'op art' painting by Jan Pienkowski entitled 'Black Cat' which accounted for 24 per cent of London sales and 13 per cent in Manchester, making it easily the most popular card in London and runner-up for popularity in Manchester. In Manchester the winner was a colour photograph of water and boats at Looe, Cornwall, which had 17 per cent of sales, though strangely enough this card accounted for only 1 per cent of sales at Claude Gill. In London second place went to a line and wash drawing of the Cutty Sark by Dennis James, which sold 19 per cent, a short lead over the third favourite which was a reproduction of Stubbs' painting 'Mares and Foals in a Landscape' (17%). Third place in Manchester went to a conventional colour drawing by M. Gear called 'Beagle Puppy' (12%) which was not sold at Claude Gill. The most popular cards were as follows:

Table 6

	London				Manchester		
Order	Card	%	% in Manchester	Order	Card	%	% in London
1	Black Cat	24	13	1	Looe, river	17	1
2	Cutty Sark	19	Under 1	2	Black Cat	13	24
3	Stubbs' horses	17	6	3	Beagle Puppy	12	Not sold
4	Two Geese	12	1	4	Holy Family	9	Not sold
5	Red Medallion	11	5	5	Head of David	8	Not sold

The Manchester percentages are generally lower because nearly twice as many cards were offered as in London, but it is interesting to see how the one card, the 'Black Cat', clearly caught people's fancy in both places, whereas other cards went well in one place but not the other. The student interviewers, in their reports on the survey, commented on the relative lack of very modern style cards in those offered and it may well be that the rather jolly black cat, covered with op art flowers, was both eye-catching and seemed to have a Christmas flavour about it. In general, the cards offered were fairly 'general purpose', mainly designed for all-the-year-round sale, but a traditional Christmas bouquet of holly and other flowers did not go particularly well. The Cutty Sark, Stubbs' horses and the picture of Looe had no Christmas connotations at all and yet they were popular in their different ways.

The Values of the Cards Bought

The surveyors recorded each separate book token by price,

even if more than one was bought by an individual customer. One secretary in London bought tokens for £76 for her employer to give as Christmas gifts, but for the most part two out of every three cards sold were of a value of £1 or less, with more of the cheaper cards sold in the larger overall total in Manchester. It was also noticeable that, although tokens could be bought in multiples of five shillings the values at a definite pound (£1, £2 and so on) were more popular.

Table 7

Value of Tokens Bought

Value	London		Manchester	
	No.	%	No.	%
5s.	11	3	56	9
10s.	76	23	179	29
15s.	29	9	59	10
£1	80	25	144	23
£1 5s. . . .	25	8	39	6
£1 10s. . . .	24	7	49	8
£1 15s. . . .	4	1	5	1
£2	48	15	48	8
£2 5s. . . .	5	2	6	1
£2 10s. . . .	5	2	4	1
£3 and under 4 . .	9	3	16	2
£4 and under 5 . .	4	1	0	—
£5 and under 6 . .	4	1	9	1
£6 and under 10 . .	1	—	0	—
£10 and over . .	1	—	0	—
Total . . .	326	100	614	100

For whom the Tokens were Bought

As this survey was carried out to try to add to the knowledge of books as gifts the recipients of the tokens were
important people. It was not possible to ask for much
detail in such a brief set of questions but it was possible to
analyse the answers in detail. Table 8 gives a large number
of categories of recipients and it can be seen that within the
basic family of husband, wife, sons and daughters purchases
for brothers or sisters are by far the most common with 13
per cent in London and 11 per cent in Manchester being
for siblings, and in both places more for brothers than
sisters. More were bought for men than women in other
cases too – more for husbands than wives, more for sons
than daughters, more for fathers than mothers. Unfortunately the analysis did not distinguish between grand-
fathers and grandmothers, uncles and aunts or nieces and
nephews; perhaps we might have found this sex difference
in these categories too. Outside the basic family, tokens for
nieces and nephews accounted for 15 per cent of London
sales and 18 per cent in Manchester. But friends accounted
for a large proportion of purchases, 29 per cent in London
and 33 per cent in Manchester, and whilst 'friends' is a
broad category it was clear that tokens are popular as
gifts from young people to their friends. Only 3 to 4 per
cent of tokens were bought as gifts for colleagues or
business associates but these few accounted for some
higher priced tokens.

We have noted how, within the family, the male
seemed to be a favoured recipient and, wherever it was
possible to distinguish the sex of the recipient without
probing this was noted. Table 9 shows how, in these

cases, men outnumbered women approximately two to
one. It is therefore apparent that book tokens are successful as gift substitutes for men, and this fits in well with
the common cry heard from women at Christmas or
birthday times, that 'men are so difficult to buy presents
for.'

Table 8

For Whom Tokens were Bought

Type of person	London		Manchester	
	No.	%	No.	%
Husband . . .	6	2	9	1
Wife	0	—	4	1
Son	5	2	18	3
Daughter . . .	1	—	3	—
Father . . .	16	2	13	2
Mother . . .	3	1	7	1
Brother . . .	26	8	45	7
Sister . . .	17	5	23	4
(Total in basic family) .	(74)	(20)	(122)	(19)
Grandparent . .	3	1	1	—
Grandchild . .	0	—	7	1
Uncle or aunt . .	8	3	4	1
Niece or nephew. .	47	15	112	18
Brother or sister-in-law	16	5	22	4
Son or daughter-in-law	2	1	9	1
Father or mother-in-law	2	1	4	1
Cousin . . .	22	7	28	5
Fiance . . .	0	—	3	—
Friend . . .	90	29	202	33
College or business associate . . .	8	3	22	4
Others . . .	41	13	78	13
Total . . .	313	100	614	100

Table 9

Sex of Recipient, where Distinguishable

				London		Manchester	
				No.	*%*	*No.*	*%*
Male .	.	.	.	109	65	218	71
Female	.	.	.	59	35	90	29
Total	.	.	.	168	100	308	100

Book or Gift?

We wanted to try to find out how purchasers regarded the book tokens and specially to try to distinguish between those people who really wanted to give a *book* but perhaps could not find the right one or were unsure of the recipient's tastes and so gave a token as a book-substitute and people who were rather stuck for ideas as to what to give as a *gift* and decided to give a book token rather than something else. The two field workers were allowed to put this rather clumsy question however they wished since we could not find a perfect wording for it. In the actual field situation it raised no problems and practically all our respondents were able to answer the question. The result was two to one in favour of 'book' in Manchester (67%) and a small majority was in favour in London (53%). As Claude Gill is in Oxford Street in the heart of a busy general shopping centre the larger 'gift' proportion is not altogether surprising and could denote a number of people who were actually lured into a bookshop for 'gift' buying who might next time actually return for 'book' buying. However, this is supposition, and it was found that 84 per cent of purchasers in London and 83 per cent in Manchester had actually bought book tokens before, leaving less than one in five who were new buyers – though this is by no means an unappreciable minority.

Numbers of Tokens Bought

Although it introduced an element of uncertainty into the replies it was felt to be worth while to ask people if they could say how many book tokens they intended buying during the Christmas period. Clearly some respondents might not know, some might overestimate and others might, later on, buy tokens they had not expected to buy. In general, though, as the questions were put

Table 10

Number of Tokens Bought at Christmas

	London		Manchester	
	No.	%	No.	%
1	177	55	241	39
2	76	24	105	17
3	40	13	81	13
4	6	2	59	10
5	12	4	29	5
6	7	2	42	7
7	0	—	34	6
8	2	1	8	1
9	0	—	0	—
10 or more . .	0	—	15	2
Total . . .	320	100	614	100

no more than ten days before Christmas we felt that most answers would be reasonably accurate. By far the largest proportions of people were buying one token only – 55 per cent in London and 39 per cent in Manchester. There were rather more multiple purchases in Manchester than London as Table 10 shows.

The Impact of Advertising

In addition to normal advertising Book Tokens Ltd had run a television campaign in the north-west in the winter of 1968 and it was felt that a question on the effects of advertising could usefully be included. All informants were asked if they had seen any advertising of book tokens before Christmas and their answers were categorised according to the various media. The bulk of purchasers, 95

Table 11

Advertising

	London		Manchester	
	No.	%	No.	%
No advertising seen .	307	95	467	76
Yes, papers and magazines only . .	6	2	46	7
Yes, television only .	0	—	69	11
Yes, papers/magazines and television . .	0	—	4	1
Yes, on buses . .	0	—	9	1
Yes, in shops . .	0	—	14	2
Yes, unspecified . .	9	3	5	1
Total . . .	322	100	614	100

per cent in London and 76 per cent in Manchester said they had seen none, but 12 per cent in Manchester did claim to have seen television commercials.

The Purchasers of the Tokens

Having looked at the tokens and the recipients we now turn to consider the purchasers themselves. Although it seemed as if more tokens were intended for men than for women the purchasers were predominantly women, with 60 per cent in London and 51 per cent in Manchester. Data on the ages of recipients was gathered only in ten-year classes – twenties, thirties etc., – and the analyses show a predominance of younger people at Claude Gill, with 45 per cent in their twenties, whilst at Sherratt & Hughes the age distribution is flatter with two minor peaks in the twenties and forties. Of course the two shops

Table 12

Age of Purchasers

	London		Manchester	
	No.	%	No.	%
Under 20 . . .	22	7	45	7
Twenties . . .	137	45	146	24
Thirties . . .	54	18	84	14
Forties . . .	49	16	154	25
Fifties . . .	24	8	116	19
Sixties . . .	15	5	35	6
Seventies . . .	3	1	29	5
Eighties . . .	0	—	1	—
Total . . .	304	100	610	100

are different in character as well as situation and one would expect more 'casual' purchasers in Oxford Street. Nevertheless the fairly high proportions of relatively young people, especially in London, indicates that book substitutes are popular with the younger adult.

Information on the social class of purchasers was obtained by asking employed people for their occupations (and in the case of housewives their husband's occupation). Details were obtained for all except eleven London respondents and the results were classified according to the Institute of Practitioners in Advertising six-point scale, and also by an empirical set of types of occupations drawn from the replies given. Even though the age structure for the two shops differed, the social class distributions were very similar. As might have been expected, the great majority of token buyers were what is generally called 'middle class' and there were few people with manual occupations amongst them. Table 13 shows all the occupations and notes 12 to 13 per cent of them as students. Table 14 analyses only those occupations classifiable by the IPA scale and compares them with the national distribution, showing that whilst neither Manchester nor London had more than 10 per cent in the C_2DE group the national proportion is 68 per cent. Table 15 then looks at some types of occupations and the large numbers in the C_1 class are illustrated by the 43 per cent of classifiable occupations in London and 34 per cent in Manchester which we called 'clerical or secretarial' or 'non-technical professional'. The proportions in the C_1 category are to some extent a function of youth, since it is to be expected that some of those people, especially men, who at present hold only

Table 13
Social Class of All Respondents

	London		Manchester	
	No.	%	No.	%
A Higher managerial, administrative or professional	23	7	65	11
B Intermediate managerial, administrative or professional . . .	86	27	167	27
C₁ Supervisory, clerical, junior managerial etc.	128	41	250	41
C₂ Skilled manual	18	6	45	7
D Semi-skilled or unskilled . . .	2	1	11	2
E Pensioners or casual workers . .	0	—	0	—
Students	42	13	76	12
Retired	3	1	0	—
Others	13	4	—	—
Total	315	100	614	100

Table 14
Social Class A to E only

	London		Manchester		England and Wales
	No.	%	No.	%	%
A	23	9	65	12	3
B	86	33	167	31	12
C₁	128	50	250	46	17
C₂	18	7	45	8	34
D	2	1	11	2	26
E	0	—	0	—	8
Total	257	100	538	100	100

fairly low grade 'white-collar' posts will eventually move up the social scale as they attain higher positions in their work. Perhaps the principal conclusion to be drawn from these analyses is the wide range of middle-class people who bought book tokens with each of the three middle-class categories being approximately represented three times more amongst token purchasers than they are in the general population.

Table 15

Occupations of Purchasers

	London		Manchester	
	No.	%	No.	%
Clerical or secretarial	51	22	108	20
Non-technical professional . . .	53	23	77	14
Student	42	18	76	14
Teacher or academic work . . .	19	8	85	16
Technical professional	27	11	56	11
Commerce, industry, managerial . .	18	8	46	9
Medical	12	5	30	6
Central or local government . . .	10	4	31	6
Shopkeeper or assistant	2	1	17	3
Clergyman	1	—	6	1
Total	235	100	532	100

Conclusions on Purchasers

It is clear from this survey, limited though its scope may be, that book tokens do have a function as book substitutes and nearly two-thirds of purchasers in the two cities were buying them in place of a *book* rather than just as a general *gift* substitute. When this is related to the prices of the tokens, however, it is found that two-thirds of tokens bought were for no more than £1, which is not very much to pay for a hardback book these days. Many of the tokens were being bought for relatives amongst whom would be included children, but nearly a third were for friends who may be assumed to be adult or near-adult. There was also the very noticeable two to one ratio of men to women as recipients and this indicates the appropriateness of tokens for people who are often regarded as 'difficult' when it comes to finding gifts for them. It can, therefore, be concluded that gift tokens fulfil a number of functions as book substitutes; they can be relatively cheap compared with the prices of actual books; they carry some of the status attached to giving books but they spare the donor the problem of actually selecting a title; they are appropriate for a wide range of people, especially friends and less close relatives such as nieces and nephews and they can be given to people of all ages, especially the young.

The Exchange of Book Tokens

The London–Manchester survey was an attempt to look at the purchase of tokens as book substitutes, but a survey was also made of the encashment of book tokens to try to find out something about what happened when their recipients used them. In this study there arose the problem that book tokens are encashed over a long period of time and we could not hope to have the information collected by our own field workers as they would have to spend long periods in the shops, often dealing with no tokens for hours or even days on end. We were very fortunate in receiving offers of co-operation from a number of bookshops who agreed to record, on duplicated forms, details of encashed book tokens. The recording dealt simply with the value of the token, the approximate age of the person (as estimated by the assistant so as not to involve them in any questioning), the sex of the person, the titles chosen, whether from stock or to order, whether in paper or cloth binding, and, where possible, an estimate of the ease or difficulty the person appeared to have had in choosing how to spend the token. The survey was carried out over a period of approximately four weeks after Easter 1968 though the period varied from shop to shop. The participants were Bowes & Bowes of Bath, Austicks (general) Bookshop of Leeds, and W. H. Smith's branches at Carlisle, Salisbury, Sutton and Walsall. Altogether 327 people were surveyed and as the people involved at each shop did not exceed sixty-eight at the most the seven shops have been put together in two sets of 'private' and 'Smith's' for presenting the results, though each shop was analysed separately when results were looked at. The result is that Bowes & Bowes and Austicks together (which will be called the 'private' bookshops) account for 109 people, exactly one-third of the total, and the four Smith's branches account for the remaining 218. It is not claimed that these shops are in any way a 'sample' of British bookshops, but at a pilot enquiry level they produce results which are suggestive and throw some further light on book tokens as gift substitutes.

The values of the tokens encashed showed again the relatively small amounts of money spent on these gifts. In the private shops 51 per cent were under £1 and at the Smith's branches the figure was 70 per cent. When the range is extended up to 30s. the percentages become 74 per cent for the private shops and 87 per cent for Smith's. The relatively low values are probably a reflection of the type of people using them. At the private shops 28 per cent of the users were estimated to be under 15, and at the Smith's shops this proportion was 45 per cent. Of course, the estimating of age can lead to great errors and one would not want these percentages to be taken as reliable, but it is clear that the assistants who made the estimates judged these proportions of token users to be 'young' people. If we add on the next group, judged to be between 15 and 24 (the young adults) these accounted for 18 per cent in the private shops and 20 per cent in Smith's. Thus 46 per cent in the private shops and 65 per cent in the Smith's shops were adjudged to be below 24 years of age. However rough these estimates may be it is clear that many token users were young and that the Smith's branches had more young people than the private shops.

The sex ratios of the token users at the two categories of shops showed strong similarities. Fifty-seven per cent of the users at the private shops and 54 per cent at the Smith's were female, which is an interesting difference from the predominance of male-intended recipients in the purchase survey. This difference may be explained by the different times of year of the two surveys and the high proportion of young people involved. The encashment survey followed the Easter buying period when it may be expected that numbers of small tokens may be bought for young people, and for this group of recipients the problem of the 'difficult man for a Christmas present' does not loom as large.

The impact of young people is reinforced by an analysis of the types of books bought with the tokens. At the Smith's branches 41 per cent of the books identifiable were children's books, and although this was only 24 per cent at the private shops there were no other comparable categories in size. Scientific and technical books accounted for 8 per cent of purchases at both types of shops, indicating that the tokens were often put to practical uses. Fiction accounted for 9 per cent at the private shops and 7 per cent at the Smith's branches, whilst reference books, atlases and maps were 10 per cent in the Smith's shops and 6 per cent in the private ones. Apart from the large proportion of children's books, however, the tokens were spread over a wide variety of types of book. And when the term 'book' is used, it may be noted that 35 per cent of the purchases at the private shops and 44 per cent at the Smith's branches were paperbacks. These high proportions were frequently accounted for by children buying two or three paperbacks with one token. Children noticeably seemed to like to get 'quantity' for their tokens, and cheap paperbacks obviously held great appeal to them. In remarking on this it should be added that the 'Ladybird' books, which were classed as hardbacks, were noted time and again and were clearly very popular with the young children. Virtually all book tokens were used for books in stock and less than one person in twenty at either of the types of shops used tokens for books ordered. The assistants also noted very few people indeed who appeared to have any great difficulty in finding purchases for their tokens, though they were greater in number at the private shops than at Smith's.

This small survey should not be taken for anything more

than an ideas-seeking study which might produce hypotheses but could not hope to test them. The encashment shops were different in type from the two used for the Christmas purchase survey and as they were surveyed at a different time of the year no addition of the one survey to to the other should be attempted. Seen by itself, the encashment survey shows how book tokens have a particularly useful function as presents for young people, especially children, and that in many cases the tokens are of a fairly low monetary value. Nevertheless the young people appear to have a tendency to shop for quantity in many cases and so cheap paperbacks do well in the using of the tokens. For adults the tokens are used for a very wide range of purchases, and one private bookseller in a university town has commented to us (outside this survey) that he has noted how frequently students come to the shop in January to buy textbooks with book tokens. Perhaps the most interesting social consequence of all which stems from the book token system is that it brings both purchasers and users into bookshops, and, particularly for children, this is often an exciting experience since it is so pleasant to have a form of credit which means that anything one buys is, in a sense, 'free'. A similar type or reaction has been noticed amongst young people in second-hand bookshops where so many of the books appear to be 'bargains' and the offer of remainders produces a reaction of this type too. 'Books as bargains' seem to have a particular attraction which would merit further investigation and book tokens can be viewed as a means whereby all the recipients are provided with the opportunity to obtain any book as a bargain – indeed free.

Conclusions on Books as Gifts

This chapter has dealt with a number of small enquiries into the function of books as gifts in our society. None of the surveys are of sufficient size or validity for drawing firm conclusions, but our resources are too limited to work beyond pilot stages. The studies do appear to indicate that books as gifts have a fairly wide range of popularity and are hearteningly popular amongst the younger generation. The older people in the Christmas gift survey mostly seemed to enjoy receiving books, and books can give satisfactions which are more deep and lasting than those derived from other sorts of gifts. Clearly the status factor should not be overlooked either. Books as gifts confer status on book donors and recipients and indicate a form of taste which associates people with 'book culture'. Book tokens, as book gift substitutes, have both a functional appeal in allowing the recipient free choice and saving the giver postage costs, and the studies of their purchase and encashment indicate that they have a popularity amongst young adults and children which must help to develop an easier association with the purchase and ownership of books amongst many people.

Chapter 3

The Book Shop and the Book Buyer

In the first report[1] on this research programme it was made clear that, from the market research and other statistical data available, it was safe to assume that book borrowers include large numbers of book buyers as well. If a person is prepared to allocate some of his scarce resources to buying books this shows a degree of loyalty and a realistic demand for the product. One can suggest various factors which affect this demand. The attitude to books learned in childhood and adolescence is one which has been discussed previously[2] and the establishment of a book-buying habit is associated with this. The effects of education are also important; anyone who undergoes a course of further education will be forced to buy at least standard textbooks and this initiation into bookshops and book buying may introduce a person to a more general pattern of book buying. A number of university booksellers have commented on the way in which a large number of their student customers are obviously not used to using a bookshop when they first come up to university but, as has been shown in past researches and from current studies de-

[1] *Books and Reading.*
[2] Ibid., Chapter 2.

scribed below, highly educated people are overrepresented amongst bookship customers. Further factors related to demand are a person's occupation and his friendship groups. In certain occupations books are 'tools of the trade' and in certain social circles books form an integral part of the group's shared interests.

The Geographical Distribution of Bookshops

This brief outline of the factors of 'demand' affecting book-buying ignores the 'supply' aspect of analysis. It is quite obvious that the two are interrelated but it would be an oversimplification to suggest that bookshops have taken root only where there is sufficient demand based on the factors outlined above.

Perhaps it is because this research has been carried out from a northern industrial city that the researchers became interested in the geographical distribution of bookshops in this country. Although the city of Sheffield, with a population of half a million, has a fair cross-section of bookshops (lacking only a branch of W. H. Smith), the neighbouring urban region of the South Yorkshire coal-field is very poorly endowed with bookshops; here the library service meets the main demand for books of all kinds, both reference and fiction. It is also interesting to note that in this area which is without bookshops there is a large number of schools with branches of Scholastic Publications' Paperback Book Clubs. The decision to investigate the national geographical distribution of bookshops was stimulated partially, therefore, by an awareness of the local situation, but also because any analysis of book buying would be incomplete which ignored the 'supply' side of the economic and social equation. An attempt was therefore made to analyse the distribution of bookshops in Britain, relating this to the distribution of population.

The basic data used for the study were the 1966 Sample Census and the 1968 list of members of the Booksellers Association, excluding from the latter list any entries where book tokens were not sold in the hope that this would remove marginal organisations belonging to the Booksellers Association for other reasons than bookselling. However, it is possible that the 'shops' drawn from the Booksellers Association list included some which were not in fact engaged in trade, so that there is probably an over-estimate of the number of 'shops' and the ratios of population to bookshops are still too generous. Another limitation in the study is that the area boundaries used in the Booksellers Association list do not always coincide with Census areas.

The analysis was done by counting the number of bookshops in each county in England, Scotland and Wales and also making a separate count of the numbers of bookshops in a number of the major towns in Britain. It must be recognised that this is inevitably a crude index, since all bookshops, no matter how large or small, good or bad, are included as equals in this count, but as no such analysis has ever been made before it is hoped that the crudity of this initial measure will be recognised and accepted for what it is. A ratio was then obtained by dividing the population of the county or the town by the number of bookshops in the relevant area thus giving an index (rounded off to the nearest thousand) of the thousands of people per bookshop for the various counties and towns.

The county analysis is given in tabular form on page 93 and in map form on page 96 and it is apparent that the county analysis produces some strange looking results with northern parts of Scotland and central Wales seeming to have the best provisions of bookshops in the country. These counties (which come in the double-hatched 1 bookshop per 3–9,000 people on the map) are mainly 'freak' results which arise from counties with very small populations where it is only necessary to have one or two small bookshops to produce a very good ratio per thousand population. The most useful map category is actually the second one, the diagonal striped 10–18,000 people per bookshop, which draws attention to the clustering of this category in the home counties and the south-east. If the third category of the horizontal stripe 19–28,000 people per bookshop is then looked at in conjunction with the 10–18,000 category a rough line from the Severn to the Wash can be seen and south-east, north-west divisions can be made. We would again stress that this county analysis cannot be anything more than a crude initial measurement which should not be taken as more than an initial picture. But, with all its limitations, the index *does* show that there is a general pattern discernible in the country, with the south and east better supplied with bookshops than the north and west.

To take the national analysis further ratios were calculated for a number of towns and cities, using as a starting point a statistical analysis of British towns carried out by two social scientists, Moser and Scott.[1] They made a study

[1] C. A. Moser and W. Scott, *British Towns, A Statistical Study of their Social and Economic Differences*, Oliver & Boyd, Edinburgh, 1961.

Geographical Distribution of Bookshops: England, Wales and Scotland – County Analysis

Ratios were calculated to give the number of thousand people to each bookshop for each county.

England

Bedfordshire	19	Hampshire	15	Shropshire	18
Berkshire	17	Isle of Wight	7	Somerset	21
Buckingham	19	Herefordshire	14	Staffordshire	49
Cambridgeshire	14	Hertfordshire	19	Suffolk	16
Cheshire	26	Huntingdon	44	Surrey	13
Cornwall	7	Kent	18	Sussex	12
Cumberland	15	Lancashire	36	Warwickshire	30
Derbyshire	33	Leicestershire	31	Westmorland	7
Devonshire	29	Lincolnshire	21	Wiltshire	19
Dorset	9	Norfolk	20	Worcestershire	29
Durham	46	Northamptonshire	17	Yorkshire-East	22
Essex	23	Northumberland	29	North	34
Gloucestershire	17	Nottinghamshire	47	West	39
Greater London Council	15	Oxfordshire	11		
		Rutland	9		

Wales

Anglesey	28	Carmarthenshire	21	Merionethshire	6
Brecon	18	Denbighshire	19	Montgomeryshire	8
Caernarvonshire	7	Flintshire	31	Pembrokeshire	24
Cardiganshire	18	Glamorgan	34	Radnorshire	6

Scotland

Aberdeenshire	21	Clackmannanshire	14	Lanarkshire	40
Angus	16	Dumfries	13	E. Lothian	18
Argyll	8	Dumbarton	52	M. Lothian	29
Ayrshire	19	Fifeshire	10	W. Lothian	51
Banff	9	Inverness-shire	10	Moray	6
Berwick	22	Kincardinshire	0	Roxburgh	22
Bute	8	Perthshire	7	Selkirk	4
Nairn	8	Renfrewshire	9	Stirling	25
Orkney & Shetland	3	Ross	19	Sutherland	0
Peebles	5	Kinross	0	Wigtownshire	28
Caithness	9	Kirkudbrightshire	5		

of 157 towns in England and Wales with populations of over 50,000 using census and other statistical data analysed by computer, 'to see to what extent one can discern a systematic pattern for all, or groups of, towns both in common and contrasting developments.' From their very intricate correlations between various quantitative data Moser and Scott found it possible to put forward three main types of towns, and within these three types various subdivisions were discernible, all derived from similarities between towns and cities thrown up by the computer comparisons.

In all there were fourteen categories, but not all of these were useful for the bookshop analysis. It was also found that recent boundary changes in the Greater London area made some comparisons with bookshop data impossible and so the third main classification which dealt largely with the outer London region was unfortunately less useful than had been hoped. Nevertheless it was possible to allocate index numbers to many towns in two of the three main categories, and these are given on p. 97–98. A low index number indicates good bookshop provision; thus the figure 8 for Eastbourne reads that Eastbourne has one bookshop per 8,000 people, whereas Blackpool has only one bookshop per 30,000 people.

In general it can be seen fairly clearly that towns and cities which Moser and Scott classify as 'Mainly Resorts, Centres of Administration and Commercial Towns' are better provided for than the 'Mainly Industrial Towns', although there are considerable differences between towns *within* the main categories and sub-categories. For example, seaside resorts and spas are generally speaking well provided with bookshops but Blackpool, Harrogate and Southend are less well provided for than some industrial towns. Clearly there are a number of special factors in every single case, but *in general* it can be said that the presence of a university in any town is likely to help the bookshop provision and so some *northern* towns appear to be helped by this. Scott and Moser's categories were based on a number of social indices, but all put together they could be said to have produced an amalgam which quantitatively describes the 'quality of life' in various towns and cities, and allying bookshop provision with this index demonstrates that the more affluent parts of the country, the areas of highest social class, the parts which are developing (as in the examples from the suburbs and suburban towns) rather than those which are in need of help, the administrative and commercial rather than the industrial and producing – all these together tend to produce a discernible general pattern of bookshop provision. However, whilst the county and the town analyses may seem to add to the stereotyped picture of civilisation being limited to south of the Wash (or even Watford in some people's minds) the analysis *is* very general indeed and any town or county can be changed by the enterprise of new booksellers opening up in areas which seem to have a lack of provision. For this reason the description given by John Prime[1] of his own venture in King's Lynn is of the greatest importance since it showed that it was possible for a man with tremendous knowledge of the book trade and indefatigable enterprise to open a completely new bookshop

[1] See 'Is there a Future for the Small Independent Bookseller?', *The Bookseller*, no. 3363, 6 June 1970.

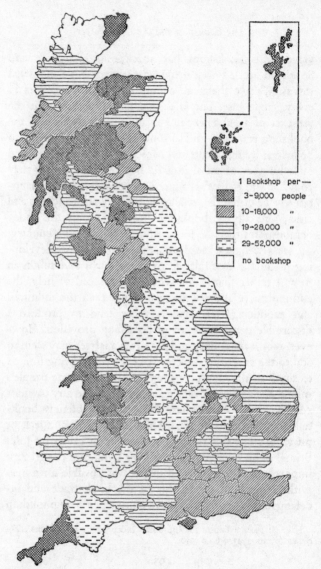

1 Bookshop per —

▨	3-9,000 people
▨	10-18,000 "
▤	19-28,000 "
▦	29-52,000 "
□	no bookshop

Map showing geographical distribution of bookshops: England, Wales and Scotland—County Analysis.

in an area which has been called 'the publishers' representatives' graveyard'. What is saddening about John Prime's

Bookshop Distribution by Types of Towns

A. *Resorts, Centres of Administration and Commercial Towns*

Seaside Resorts		Spas, administrative centres		Commercial centres with some industries	
Eastbourne	8	Cambridge	6	York	10
Worthing	10	Oxford	7	Lancaster	12
Bournemouth	13	Bath	8	Southampton	13
Brighton	15	Bedford	8	Worcester	14
Southport	16	Colchester	11	Norwich	15
Hastings	18	Poole	24	Ipswich	15
Blackpool	30	Harrogate	30	Lincoln	15
		Southend	42	Reading	16
				Bristol	17
				Northampton	21
				Portsmouth	25
				Great Yarmouth	26

B. *Industrial Towns*

Traditional Railway Centres		Textile Centres, Yorkshire and Lancashire	
Derby	18	Leeds	19
Carlisle	18	Manchester	21
Chesterfield	18	Leicester	22
Barrow	21	Blackburn	25
Wakefield	22	Burnley	26
Swindon	23	Nottingham	28
Doncaster	25	Bradford	29
Stockport	35	Halifax	31
Coventry	36	Bury	31
Newcastle-under-Lyme	36	Oldham	33
Sheffield	37	Huddersfield	37
Mansfield	38	Bolton	38
		Rochdale	87

Ports and Black Country Towns		N.E. Seaboard	
Newcastle-on-Tyne	14	South Shields	21
Grimsby	19	West Hartlepool	26
Liverpool	25	Sunderland	47
Wolverhampton	32	Gateshead	99
Birmingham	38		
Hull	42		

C. *Suburbs and Suburban Type Towns*

The majority of the towns which Scott and Moser analysed in this group are now part of the Greater London Council and changes of boundaries make comparisons virtually impossible.

The overall ratio for the Greater London Council is 15.

The following towns are not affected by changes:

Slough	15	Gosport	33
Luton	22	Gillingham	40

conclusion is that the very narrow profit margins that booksellers must accept today requires a new bookseller to have a dedication to his work which is *not* reasonably rewarded in financial terms.

The Bookshop and its Customers

During the programme of research in the academic session 1968–69 two surveys were made of the customers of bookshops. In November 1968 a one-week survey of the customers of Dillon's University Bookshop, Malet Street, London[1], was carried out, and in March 1969 a one-week study was made of the customers of A. B. Ward's, Chapel Walk, Sheffield. Clearly these are two quite different bookshops, Dillon's being a very large

[1] The costs of this survey were borne by Dillon's Bookshop and we are grateful for their support and cooperation in this study.

London bookshop mainly (but by no means wholly) devoted to university bookselling, whilst Ward's is a centre-of-town provincial bookshop, much smaller in size. Dillon's is a shop of some 16,000 square feet floor space normally holding a stock of about £230,000 in value, whilst Ward's has just under 1,000 square feet of floor space and has a stock of approximately £22,500 value.

The two surveys were not intended to be direct comparisons, although a number of similar questions were asked of customers at both the shops, but rather the emphasis in the Dillon's survey was on the reactions of the customers to what is generally regarded as one of the top university bookshops in the country. The Dillon's survey therefore assumed that the customers were likely to be fairly sophisticated well-educated people whose wants were mainly in the academic field. The Ward's survey was of a much less specific nature since although it is a general bookshop in a large city of half a million population, no particular assumptions about the customers could be made apart from an expectation that they would be likely to reflect general results from surveys of book readers which had pointed to book readers being better educated and of higher social class than the general population. The Ward's survey therefore looked much more closely at the customer as a person and more questions were asked of respondents about their general involvement in the world of books.

In both surveys the interviews were carried out throughout the day from Monday to Saturday inclusive with interviews at regular intervals all through the day, though with attempts to have more interviews done at busy times so as to keep the sampling fairly representative of the people in the shop at any given time. All respondents were stopped and asked for the interview as they were leaving the shop and refusals were very few apart from people who were in a great hurry to get to lectures, catch buses etc. The Dillon's survey was done by four specially employed women with interviewing experience with Miss Burgoyne, the research assistant, acting as general super-visor and fifth interviewer. The Sheffield interviews were carried out by seven university students chosen for the job and paid for this work during their vacation. At Dillon's 646 successful interviews were obtained and at Ward's, the smaller shop, the number was 340. All results were coded and analysed by ICL punch cards.

In the following sections of results the first section presents some basic characteristics of the customers at the two shops and in this section comparisons are given. In the second section Dillon's is looked at as a large London university bookshop and in the third section Ward's is looked at as a middle-sized provincial general bookshop.

Dillon's and Ward's Customers: Basic Characteristics
At both bookshops there was a predominance of male customers with Dillon's having slightly more men than Ward's. This result would seem to fit in with a general pattern of men predominating in most previous surveys of books and readers.

All respondents were categorised by age, although in the first survey (at Dillon's) the lowest category was simply 'under 20', whilst at Ward's an 'under 16' category

Table 16
Sex of Customers

	Dillon's		Ward's	
	No.	%	No.	%
Male	415	66	209	61
Female	218	34	131	39
Not recorded	(13)	—	—	—
Total	646	100	340	100

was added. Table 16 shows very clearly how relatively young the customers of both bookshops were, 45 per cent of Dillon's and 49 per cent of Ward's customers being under 25 years of age. In some ways the relative youthfulness of the customers might be expected at Dillon's, although university staff and casual customers could easily add more age, but at Ward's the youthfulness came as something of a surprise, albeit a very heartening one. Of course, these data merely reflect the people who had been in the bookshops and were interviewed on leaving them; although the respondents are called 'customers' this does not mean that they had all *bought* books, as Table 23 will show. Nevertheless this analysis of age is important since it shows that two important bookshops do have large proportions of young people visiting them, and the old-fashioned image of the bookshop as a somewhat fusty and dusty place largely visited by old ladies in funny hats and old men in long mackintoshes should now be relegated to the realms of out-of-date fiction. Relative youthfulness was also reflected in the marital status of the customers, with 37 per cent at Dillon's married and 38 per cent at Wards.

Table 17

Age of Customers

	Dillon's		Ward's	
	No.	%	No.	%
Under 16 . . . . . . {	113	18	10	3
16–20			85	25
21–24	176	27	73	21
25–34	190	29	56	16
35–44	93	14	51	15
45–54	46	7	28	8
55–64	22	2	22	6
65+	5	1	15	4
No answer	1	—	0	—
Total	646	100	340	100

Obviously it would be expected that large numbers of Dillon's customers would be students, and half of them did turn out to be full-time students. What was unexpected, especially in a survey carried out during university vacation, was that 36 per cent of the customers at Ward's were full-time students, less than a quarter of these being at school. Two points arise from these analyses. Firstly Dillon's has an interesting balance of customers with half of them full-time students and half not; of those people who were not students 27 per cent were university staff of one kind or another. But this still leaves a good proportion of Dillon's customers as not at the time directly or mainly involved in full-time higher education. It should be noted that Dillon's size and range of books makes it a very good *general* bookshop as well as one which is famous for its educational stock. The second point is that Ward's is a *general* bookshop of limited size in the town centre, and there are two bookshops (one of them a Ward's branch) at the university providing particularly for the needs of higher education students. If it is accepted that the Ward's shop surveyed provides relatively little in the way of educational books then the proportion of students in the shop reflects a *general* interest in books rather than a seeking for 'work' books.

Table 18

Student/Non-Student Status

	Dillon's		Ward's	
	No.	%	No.	%
Full-time students	322	50	121	36
Part-time student	63	10	7	2
Not a student	260	40	212	62
No answer	1	—	—	—
Total	646	100	340	100

The students (both full and part-time) were asked at what institutions they were studying and Table 19 gives this analysis. Again it is interesting to see the expected high proportions of university students at Dillon's and the rather unexpectedly high proportions at Ward's. Part-time students were more important in London because of the proximity of Birkbeck College and the London University Institute of Education, both of which added to the university numbers. Over a third of the Dillon's student customers were postgraduates and all the students were widely spread amongst faculties and subjects.

Table 19

Type of Students

			Dillon's		Ward's	
			No.	%	No.	%
University	.	.	280	73	65	51
Other colleges	.	.	105	27	37	29
School	.	.	0	—	26	20
Total	.	.	385	100	128	100

Those people who were not students were analysed for their occupations and since part-time students were usually working for their living they too were included in this analysis. Both bookshops had far higher proportions of people in the higher social status occupations than the national proportions give, and, not unexpectedly, Dillon's had an overall higher social status clientele than Ward's. The area in which Dillon's shop stands is very much an educational and commercial one and the high social status of the 'working' customers is not surprising. At Ward's the C_1 category of lower grade white-collar occupations is to some extent a reflection of the youth of some respondents who will eventually rise to higher level occupations as they grow older, but it was interesting to see at Ward's that 13 per cent of non-student customers were in the C_2 category, which is skilled manual occupations, and this must be regarded as a heartening sign to some extent of the breakdown of the 'bookshop barrier' which is believed to deter working-class people from frequenting bookshops.

Table 20

Social Status of Non-Students

	Dillons'		Ward's		National
	No.	%	No.	%	%
A Higher managerial, administrative, professional	43	13	23	10	3
B Intermediate managerial, administrative, professional	172	53	43	20	12
C₁ Supervisory, clerical, junior managerial etc.	83	26	92	42	17
C₂ Skilled manual	5	2	27	12	34
D Semi-skilled or unskilled manual	3	1	5	2	26
E Pensioners and casual workers	—	—	—	—	8
Housewives	11	3	20	9	
Unemployed	1	—	—	—	
No answer	6	2	9	4	
Total	324	100	219	100	100

The differences between the Dillon's and Ward's non-students is also clearly illustrated by an analysis of their educational backgrounds. At Dillon's almost exactly two-thirds of the working customers had a university background whilst at Ward's this was only 18 per cent (which compares interestingly with the numbers of their customers at university). The relatively high proportion of customers with elementary or secondary modern backgrounds at Ward's fits in with the greater proportions of working-class people and reinforces the picture of a fairly wide spread of customers at this shop.

Table 21

Educational Background of Non-Student Customers

	Dillon's		Ward's	
	No.	%	No.	%
University	212	65	39	18
Teacher training college. . . .	11	3	15	7
Technical, secretarial, art, etc., college .	32	10	27	12
Grammar or comprehensive school .	31	10	68	31
Elementary or secondary modern . .	15	5	57	26
No answer or unclassifiable . . .	23	7	13	6
Total	324	100	219	100

Activities of the Customers at Dillon's and Ward's

In both surveys an early question in the interview was one asking the respondent his or her reasons for the visit to the bookshop. Answers given covered a wide range from sheltering from the rain to hoping to make a date with a female assistant, but it was possible to distinguish between the two important categories of hoping actually to buy a book and just calling in to look around. Where a customer had called in to deal with an order that was classified separately. The table shows that the reasons for calling at the two shops were very similar, with over half the customers hoping to buy and over a third just coming to look round.

Table 22

Principal Reasons for Visit

	Dillon's		Ward's	
	No.	%	No.	%
Hoping to buy from stock . . .	372	56	193	56
To have a look round . . .	231	38	119	35
To deal with an order for a book . .	38	7	24	7

Note:—As these are examples from a range of reasons, of which any respondent could have more than one, percentaging is based on numbers of respondents and no gross total is given.

Having asked customers for the main reasons for their visits to the bookshops the interviewers then went on to enquire about the purchases (if any) that they had made. Those people who did buy books were asked if the books they had bought were 'intended' or 'impulse' buys, and again ordering books was analysed as a separate category.

Table 23

Principal Reasons for Visit

	Dillon's		Ward's	
	No.	%	No.	%
Bought book or books sought . .	266	41	81	24
Bought book or books on impulse .	102	16	35	10
Collected an order	15	2	12	4
Placed an order	16	2	9	3
Did not buy or order	278	43	212	62

Since each person could both buy a book they had been looking for and *also* buy a book on impulse the percentaging is again based on the total number of respondents and percentages thus exceed 100.

It is interesting to compare some of the points which emerge from the two preceding tables. At Dillon's 56 per cent of the customers had come into the shop hoping to buy from stock and 41 per cent had actually bought books during their visit, whilst at Ward's the comparative figures were 56 per cent and 24 per cent. This is an interesting reflection on the size and stocks of the two shops. Dillon's is one of the biggest bookshops in the country and is well known for its large stocks of books, particularly in academic subjects. Ward's is a much smaller general bookshop which holds a very good stock of books so far as the limitations of space permit. But it is clear that the larger the stock the higher the proportions of customers will be who do buy. Alongside this though, it is interesting to note that whilst Dillon's has 16 per cent of customers buying on impulse, Ward's is not very far behind with 10 per cent, which would seem to show that even with Ward's limited space they do have a good 'impulse buy' stock. Perhaps the most depressing figure for booksellers is the very small number of people who appear to have ordered books. If one deducts the numbers of people who bought books they were looking from the numbers who had come in hoping to buy from stock the figure for Dillon's is 106 and for Ward's 112. Yet at the two shops only 16 and 9 people respectively placed orders. Of course it does not necessarily follow that the would-be purchasers are lost to the book trade as a whole and the figures above must cover many people who went to other bookshops, who were perhaps prepared to wait for a book to come into stock or many other reasons. But the proportions of people ordering to would-be buyers who did not buy do, on the face of it, appear to be very small, and they may be a reflection of bookshop customers' lack of willingness to wait weeks, or even months, for a book that is not in stock. Neither Dillon's nor Ward's makes (as yet) any extra charge for ordering books so this cannot be a financial disincentive to ordering. With the surveys showing so many young people amongst the customers however, and these young people being accustomed to obtaining gramophone records very quickly indeed, it does seem that the book trade's general inability to deliver single-copy orders quickly may be losing the book-shops a great deal of business simply because people are not prepared to wait for orders. Much of this is speculation based on relatively crude figures from the two surveys, but whether a person wanting a book for a gift is prepared to wait an unspecified period of time for delivery when birthdays and anniversaries are immutable is open to question.

Excluding books not in stock that were ordered, the great bulk of those people who did make purchases bought only one book during the visit to the bookshop. People who bought several books were more common at Dillon's than at Ward's, which is again a reflection of the wide range of books in stock.

Since the two bookshops were so dissimilar it is not possible to make meaningful comparisons of people's activities inside the shops, but some points may be noted

Table 24

Number of Books Bought by Customers

	Dillon's		Ward's	
	No.	%	No.	%
Bought none . .	294	46	212	62
Bought one book .	205	32	93	26
Bought two books .	73	11	20	6
Bought three books .	30	5	8	2
Bought four books .	17	3	2	1
Bought five books .	7	1	2	1
Bought six or more .	17	3	2	1
Not answered . .	3	—	1	—
Total . . .	646	100	340	100

concerning the most popular sections of them. In both surveys respondents were asked what sections or parts of the bookshop they had visited and it was very noticeable how frequently the paperback sections were mentioned. Dillon's has a separate Penguin bookshop on the mezzanine floor which was visited by 14 per cent of respondents, and 16 per cent of customers said that they had looked at the general paperback section on the ground floor. Ward's has a long and attractive paperback fitment on the right of the entrance which was looked at by 26 per cent of visitors. It does seem apparent that the paperback section of a bookshop is very important indeed since it not only helps to attract people into the shop if it is near the entrance, but it also helps the visitor to establish a base within the shop from which he can then proceed once he has got his bearings and has gained sufficient confidence to move further into the shop. This points, of course, to the attraction of the rows of face-up paperbacks clearly displayed and arranged in meaningful categories and also to the need for clear sign-posting and labelling of the other parts of the shop so as to guide customers to the other sections. Customers in Dillon's have numerous interests catered for by the specialist departments though the English literature and language sections were very well visited (19%) and history, biography and archaeology also did well (14%). At Ward's the second most popular section, somewhat surprisingly, was technical subjects and science (17%), which indicates a very practical interest in books, whilst general fiction came next (14%) and sports, travel, guides and maps was fourth with 13 per cent. In general Dillon's most visited categories of books indicated a tendency for 'cultural' browsing, whilst Ward's customers seemed rather more 'practical' in the sections they visited.

At this point the parallel data for the two shops came to an end since, as was explained earlier, the two studies were carried out with rather different perspectives on the two shops. From here on the two bookshops are looked at separately, Dillon's mainly as a *university* bookshop in the metropolis and Ward's as a *general* provincial bookshop with more general customers.

Dillon's University Bookshop in London

If a number of knowledgeable people were asked to name the half-dozen best bookshops in the country it would be surprising if many of them omitted to include Dillon's. In general discussions with many people in the world of books

Dillon's has nearly always been mentioned not only with respect but also with affection. In the survey at Dillon's 75 per cent of the people questioned said that Dillon's was their *main London* bookshop, and of those who did not name Dillon's over a third said they had no main bookshop at all. Twenty-eight per cent of respondents were able to name bookshops that they thought were better than Dillon's (though some were outside London) but in many cases these other bookshops were better in the respondents' opinions because they were better for particular subjects. Dillon's was particularly commended for its large stock and wide range of books, its good location (particularly for many university people), the good service of its staff and for the particular merits of specialist departments of the shop.

With so many student customers many of the people surveyed had not been customers at Dillon's for very long, and just over a quarter said they had been customers under a year. Nevertheless it was interesting to note that the high proportion of student customers did not make Dillon's only a 'textbook repository'. Sixty-eight per cent of all customers said they bought all or most of their books for work or study from Dillon's, but 39 per cent said they bought all or most of their books *not* connected with work or study there too. The shop was also used for buying books as gifts by 12 per cent of customers 'often' and a further 32 per cent 'sometimes', which meant that virtually half the respondents found Dillon's stock appropriate for gift purchases.

In general Dillon's customers were very satisfied with the shop and found that it compared well with other bookshops in London and elsewhere. Eighty-four per cent of respondents said that they had, at one time or another, asked a member of the staff for assistance and had found them helpful; only 11 people out of 646 had any criticisms to make of the staff and many, many more commented spontaneously on their friendliness and helpfulness. In a large and busy shop such as Dillon's it could be difficult to locate an assistant but 81 per cent of respondents said that the assistants were easy to find, though one man's comment that he always located them by their beards must be puzzling for the female staff in the shop.

Since Dillon's is a shop which has grown from a merging of shops and has many ups and downs on its various floors it is not the sort of shop that a modern architect would design from scratch on his drawing board. For some customers this was clearly an attraction: a number of people mentioned the charm of the various departments all over the place and felt that this helped to give a good bookshop 'atmosphere'. In spite of Dillon's great size 20 per cent of customers would like to see even more space and 13 per cent of them confessed that they did find it rather difficult to find their way about (a matter which has received attention since the survey.) But it was clear that bookshop customers themselves hold very conflicting views and whilst one person may feel that the layout of a particular department is confusing, another may say, as one man did, 'I *like* bookshops where I can't find my way around. I come in to browse and I like it vaguely chaotic and *not* like a supermarket.' Thus it might be concluded that in a bookshop such as Dillon's, catering for a well-educated and very knowledgeable clientele, it is probably wise (and even attractive) to allow, or even deliberately arrange, a certain element of untidiness here and there which helps produce the right atmosphere for this sort of bookshop.

A. B. Ward's Bookshop in Sheffield

As has already been stressed, the two bookshop surveys were not designed to be comparative studies apart from certain fairly basic details since the two shops are of a different type, size and location. Whilst the Dillon's survey looked rather more at the shop and its particular function as a large London university bookshop the Sheffield survey used Ward's bookshop as an example of a reasonably typical provincial bookshop catering for the *general* needs of the *general* public in a large provincial city. Also the Ward's survey was carried out simultaneously with a one-week survey of the users of the Sheffield Central Public Library and in both these surveys the emphasis was more on the *people* using the two institutions rather than the bookshop and the library themselves. In the next chapter details are given of the library users, and some comparisons with the bookshop users are made, but for the final part of this chapter the focus is upon a few particular details of Ward's bookshop itself.

The interviewers recorded details of all the books bought by the respondents and these were analysed in a number of ways. An attempt was made to arrange the books bought into a limited number of categories, though the wide range of purchases made this difficult and eventually only 141 out of 187 books bought could be analysed. These give the following distribution:—

The fact that so many books were unclassified, and yet the spread within the categories used was so broad, emphasises the very *general* nature of the sales made in this

Table 25

Type of Book Bought

	No.	%
Textbooks, 'educational' .	25	18
Travel, guides, maps, etc. .	22	16
Practical, hobbies, sport .	19	13
Children's books . .	18	13
Literature, poetry, drama .	18	13
General fiction . .	13	9
Art, the arts, architecture .	12	9
History, current affairs .	8	6
Light fiction (detective, romance, etc.) . . .	6	4
Total	141	100

general bookshop and must draw attention to the fantastic range of demands made upon the ordinary general bookseller. The image that literary people may have of the bookshop as an oasis of high culture in a severely practical world is quite erroneous and the general bookseller who was only interested in selling the great works of literature would rapidly be out of business. Table 25 really stresses the point of the sociological model on page 9 that books cover a very wide range of interests and many of these interests are concerned with work and practical leisure activities.

A further factor that affects the bookseller and the

customer is the price of books. With high overheads, selective employment tax and high costs involved in orders for single copies many booksellers make very small profits these days, yet (contrary to most publishers' views) a lot of customers feel that books are high in price. The Ward's survey was able to include the prices of most books actually bought and Table 26 shows for 160 books how little money was actually spent on the great bulk of books bought in the shop. Of course, it must be recognised that most bookshops do a great deal of trade directly with libraries and in supplying education authorities with school books. Were it not for these sales (which, it should be noted, require the bookseller to give the purchasers a special discount) many booksellers would be very hard pressed to keep their shops open. It is therefore very disturbing for booksellers that the Sheffield Education Committee has recently attempted to begin the purchase of books direct from publishers, thereby depriving Sheffield booksellers of a basic source of income from a service which it has never been denied that they fulfil well. Fortunately for the booksellers a number of powerful publishers have refused to cooperate with the Education Committee, though it must have shocked the booksellers to find that a number of publishers were quite willing to agree to this by-passing of the conventional retailer. Table 26 is therefore of some importance in this context since it should be noted that many shop sales are of low monetary value and without the conventional library and school sales the ordinary shop customer would probably find himself with fewer bookshops.

Of the books bought virtually three-quarters (74%) had

Table 26

Prices of Books Bought

	No.	%
Up to 5s.	62	39
5s. and under 10s. . .	43	27
10s. and under 15s. . .	16	10
15s. and under £1 . .	6	4
£1 and under £1 10s.. .	22	14
£1 10s. and under £2. .	6	4
£2 and under £2 10s.. .	2	1
£2 10s. and under £3. .	1	1
£3 and over . . .	2	1
Total	160	100

been bought for the purchaser himself (or herself) which leaves a quite appreciable proportion of a quarter bought for someone else. Of these others for whom the books were bought, 40 per cent were children, 14 per cent were parents and 11 per cent were brothers or sisters. It would seem therefore that the slogan recently suggested by the Director of the National Book League 'Buy a Book next Present' might well be directed particularly at people looking for presents for children and also at people buying for their relations. It is also of interest to note that the high proportions of children or people related to the gift giver fit in with the idea of books being appropriate gifts for children in general, and appropriate for adults if the donor knows the recipient's tastes well enough to be able to choose an appropriate book.

Clearly the buying of books over a very wide range, as the survey shows, entailed a great deal of picking and

choosing and it was therefore not surprising to find that
for a third of the books bought the purchasers had actually
enlisted the help of a shop assistant during the course of the
choosing. This one-third of the actual books bought
entailing help from the assistants reinforces the importance
of helpful and well-trained staff who are readily available
when needed, yet equally well able to leave people to
browse when they are not required. Of course many
customers use several bookshops in the town, but it was
interesting to see that a quarter of the people interviewed
claimed Ward's to be their main bookshop to the extent
of rarely buying from any other and a further third said
they only used one other bookshop, even though Sheffield
has at least another seven.

All the respondents were asked if they were or ever had
been members of book clubs and a surprisingly high
proportion of 10 per cent said that they were now members
of a book club and another 19 per cent said that they had
been a member once but were no longer. The general
survey of a sample of the whole population made in 1965
by European Research Consultants gave only 3.3 per cent
of their respondents as members of book clubs and the
present survey gives bookshop customers as three times
that figure. This may therefore throw light on the point
frequently discussed in the book world as to whether
book clubs reduce people's book buying overall or,
contrarily, add to the total book market. The relatively
high proportions of Ward's customers who belonged to,
or had belonged to, book clubs and certainly the wide
range of book clubs mentioned, with the emphasis on the
more *general* book clubs, would suggest that once people

begin to own books of their own then the book-buying habit spreads from the club to the conventional shop.

The survey respondents were also asked if they had ever bought books after having borrowed a copy from the library and 41 per cent of them said they had done so. The types of books they had bought after borrowing were categorised and although general fiction came out as the main category (and *Lord of the Rings* was mentioned more than any other book) nevertheless the spread of books was very wide and included history, travel, education, art, literature and various practical interests.

It can thus be seen that both book clubs and libraries help to bring people into the world of books and it would thus seem most sensible to take the view that any contact with books, from no matter what source they may be obtained, helps to increase people's interest in books and their desire to own books for themselves. In the next chapter we look in more detail at some aspects of the Ward's customers' involvement in the world of books, particularly using comparisons with the people who were interviewed in the library survey.

Conclusions

This chapter has dealt with the bookshop and the book-shop customer by drawing from surveys of two very different bookshops, Dillon's University Bookshop in central London and Ward's general bookshop in central Sheffield. But in spite of the great differences between the shops themselves it has been shown that they both draw upon a relatively young, well-educated and high social status clientele. It was encouraging to see that young people support both shops so well, and it would be pleasant to think that the increasing educational facilities for young people were also creating a nation of book-lovers. Unfortunately the picture is not as rosy as it might be, since surveys made of the book buying habits of university students (who at present receive grants of £38 a year specially for books and stationery) indicate that about £12 a year on books is the average spending. And in the Parry Report on University Libraries in 1967[1] a national survey of student book buying gave the depressing statistic of an average of only six books being bought by third-year students, with 10 per cent of them buying no books at all. Clearly then the younger generation, even those in higher education, contains a large number who actively agree with Somerset Maugham's aphorism, 'It is astonishing how many books I find there is no need for me to read at all.'

But the surveys have indicated that bookshops do give great pleasure to many people. Dillon's University Book-shop is clearly a very important part of the university area in Bloomsbury and it provides specialist and general book facilities for a very wide range of students and non-students, the great bulk of whom are very appreciative of the stocks of books they can examine and the help they get from the shop assistants. Ward's in Sheffield has in many ways a more difficult task in trying to provide a *general* range of books in a smaller space for a broader spectrum of the population. Clearly it is bound to lose sales because of its space limitations, yet within those

---

[1] University Grants Committee, *Report of the Committee on Libraries* (Parry Report), HMSO, London, 1967.

limitations it does an excellent job of providing for the work, hobbies and leisure interests of people of all ages and social class.

The most important point that arises from these studies of the two bookshops is the recognition of the extremely difficult task that faces the modern bookshop in a time when there are 30,000 new titles coming on to the market each year and the bookshop customer (who is probably unaware of this flood of books) still feels aggrieved if the one copy he wants is not in stock or cannot be obtained (without charge) in a couple of days. These problems of distribution, coupled with the rapid increases in book costs, must endanger the currently good relationship which appears to exist between bookshop and customer.

Chapter 4

The Library and the Book Borrower

Introduction

This chapter deals with the results from a survey of the borrowers from the Sheffield Central Lending Library in Surrey Street carried out during the same week as the survey of the customers of A. B. Ward's bookshop in Chapel Walk not very far away. The same interviewers who did the bookshop interviews carried out the library ones, working on a rota which enabled them to move between the library and the bookshop both for a change of interviewing and also to cover busy periods at both places. Users of the library were asked for the interview as they left the adult lending section of the library building. Since the whole building contains reference libraries and an art gallery care was taken to ensure that only people who had actually been to the lending library were stopped by stationing the interviewers by the one public exit from this library. Although the lending library does not in itself include a children's section nevertheless a few fairly young people borrowing more adult books are by no means uncommon and some of them came into the sample.

The Ward's bookshop and the library interview schedules were designed to provide a certain amount of comparative information so that much of this chapter gives parallel information from the Ward's survey. In some cases, as for the basic characteristics of the library users and the bookshop customers, this means that the Ward's results are given again, but in these cases they are used to give a comparison between borrowers and buyers. In a further section on the visit to the library the tables give only library survey information, but in further sections comparisons are again possible with the bookshop customers and these deal with library borrowing, book buying and general involvement in the world of books. The intention of this chapter is, then, to look at certain aspects of the book borrower but to make the details of the borrower more interesting and more enlightening by providing comparisons with the bookshop customer wherever possible.

Characteristics of the Library Users

There were more men than women borrowers, but as Table 27 shows the male predominance at the library was rather less than it was in the bookshop.

Table 27

Sex

				Library		Ward's	
				No.	%	No.	%
Male .	.	.	.	278	55	209	61
Female	.	.	.	232	45	131	39
Total	.	.	.	510	100	340	100

The library users had a smaller proportion of married people amongst them than had the bookshop sample. At the library 32 per cent were married compared with 38 per cent at Ward's. It was therefore slightly surprising to find that with fewer married people at the library the age structure was slightly more middle-aged. Unfortunately no separate category for widowed people was included in either survey; if there had been, some of the older library people might well have turned out to be widowed. Table 28 shows over a quarter of both library and bookshop users to be under 20 years of age, but 29 per cent of library users are 45 or over compared to only 20 per cent at the bookshop.

Table 28

Age

	Library		Ward's	
	No.	%	No.	%
Under 16 . . .	21	4	10	3
16–20. . . .	118	23	85	25
21–24. . . .	75	15	73	21
25–34. . . .	78	15	56	16
35–44. . . .	69	14	51	15
45–54. . . .	52	10	28	8
55–64. . . .	52	10	22	6
65+	45	9	15	4
Total . . .	510	100	340	100

If all those people under 25 are compared, the library has 42 per cent to the bookshop's 49 per cent and so the lower proportion of students at the library is understandable. There are 24 per cent full-time students at the library compared with 36 per cent at Ward's. This comparison should not be misinterpreted: the Central Library has several *reference* sections from which books cannot be borrowed and many students of all types use these specialist libraries for reference and study. The survey here described was only of people using the *lending* library, though this does, of course, offer for loan a complete range of serious non-fiction.

Table 29

Student/Non-Student Status

	Library		Ward's	
	No.	%	No.	%
Full-time student .	122	24	121	36
Part-time student .	12	2	7	2
Not student . .	376	74	212	62
Total . . .	510	100	340	100

Table 30 looks in more detail at the types of students using the two places and the differences are quite marked. Only just over a fifth of the library-user students are at university compared to just over a half of the bookshop students. As a result, the library has higher proportions of students at other colleges of further and higher education and at school. It has been mentioned that these surveys were carried out in the Easter vacation and therefore it was not necessarily vacation for other colleges and certainly not for schools. One possible explanation of the high university proportion at the bookshop is that *being* university vacation, students at *other* universities who were home on vacation in Sheffield were making 'holiday visits' to their local general bookshop. Table 32 gives nothing like the educational differences between people in the library and bookshop who had *completed* their education, so some special factor must be assumed to have occurred to produce this particular student difference.

Table 30

Types of Students

			Library		Ward's	
			No.	%	No.	%.
University	.	.	30	22	65	51
Other colleges	.	.	54	40	37	29
School	.	.	45	34	26	20
No answer	.	.	5	4	0	—
Total	.	.	134	100	128	100

The next two tables give analyses of the occupational types of people who were not full-time students and also their educational background. Table 31 shows the library having fewer people in the AB category, 12 per cent compared to the bookshop 25/30 per cent, which indicates a higher social status amongst bookshop customers which confirms previous general studies of library and bookshop users. The library has a higher proportion of C_1 people, but neither library nor bookshop has as much as 20 per cent of the C_2DE (working class) category. Of course it must be recognised that the library surveyed was the *central* library and many people may well be satisfied with the provisions of their local branch libraries, with which Sheffield is well provided. Table 32, which gives details of the educational background of the people who have completed their education shows the library and bookshop virtually equal for proportions educated at grammar schools, but the bookshop, as expected, has more people who were at university or college – although the preponderance is not as great as might have been expected. These tables, taken together with the preceding ones which give data on the student users, reinforce the apparent importance of

Table 31

Social Status of Non-Students

	Library		Ward's	
	No.	%	No.	%
A Higher managerial, administrative, professional	11	3	23	10
B Intermediate managerial, administrative professional . . .	36	9	43	20
C_1 Supervisory, clerical, junior managerial, etc..	196	51	92	42
C_2 Skilled manual . . .	53	14	27	12
D Semi-skilled or unskilled manual .	14	4	5	2
E Casual workers	2	1	0	—
Housewives	38	10	20	9
'Retired' only answer . . .	34	9	0	—
No answer	4	1	9	4
Total	388	100	219	100

education (and especially higher and further education) in bringing adolescent and young adult people into the book world. This point may seem to have been made so many times now that it may be becoming blunted, but its importance cannot be ignored.

Table 32

Educational Background of Non-Students

	Library		Ward's	
	No.	%	No.	%
University	51	13	39	18
Teacher training college. . .	24	6	15	7
Technical, secretarial, art, etc., college .	33	9	27	12
Grammar or comprehensive school .	126	32	68	31
Elementary or secondary modern school .	149	38	57	26
No answer or unclassifiable . . .	5	1	13	6
Total	388	100	219	100

The tables and commentary given so far have drawn attention to the similarities and differences between the two samples of people interviewed at the library and the bookshop. The next section deals with the library users alone and gives details of the activities in which they engaged during their visit to the library.

The Visit to the Library

All the people interviewed were asked the reason for their visit to the library and Table 33 gives classifications for all the types of answers. As might have been expected the bulk of people had been to return books and borrow some more (58%) but it was slightly surprising to find nearly a quarter coming only to borrow and not to return books. The 4 per cent of people visiting the record library were people who, in doing so, had to pass through the lending library area.

Table 33

Purpose of Visit

	No.	%
To return and borrow books .	296	58
To borrow books . .	116	23
To renew books . . .	50	10
To return books . . .	33	6
To have a look round . .	25	5
To use the record library .	22	4
To look up something .	8	2
To collect a book on order .	6	1
To join the library . .	4	1
To meet someone . .	1	0
Total no. of people . .	510	—

Note:—Percentage total exceeds 100 as some people gave more than one reason.

The library users were next asked a series of questions about the books which they had borrowed, if they did actually borrow. Fifty-nine people (12%) had not borrowed any books at all. Of those people who did borrow the largest proportion, just under a third, borrowed two books, and roughly speaking a quarter borrowed one or three.

It was possible to gain detailed information about 1,045 books borrowed and these were analysed first of all according to a number of types. As Table 35 shows, just

Table 34

Number of Books Borrowed (Borrowers only)

	No.	%
Borrowed one book . .	127	28
Borrowed two books . .	151	33
Borrowed three books .	112	25
Borrowed four books . .	34	8
Borrowed five books . .	18	4
Borrowed six books . .	6	1
Borrowed seven books. .	3	1
Total	451	100

over a half of all the books borrowed were fiction and the next popular category was scientific and technical books (17%) with no other category reaching 10 per cent. Of course it must be remembered that this survey was at the *central* library where any borrower in the city can go and where people may particularly go if they are looking for a good range of books on specialist topics. The diversity of borrowing thus may be taken to reflect the range of interests catered for by this library. Later in the survey interview each respondent was asked what sort of books he or she *usually* borrowed from the library. As the second column shows, people tended to *say* that they borrowed more non-fiction than they actually *had* borrowed in the study.

The respondents were asked, for each book actually borrowed, if it had been chosen for borrowing because of its specific title, or if it was in a specific subject or, if neither of these, if it was 'just something to read'. Since

Table 35

Types of Books Borrowed

		Actually borrowed		Said to be borrowed	
		No.	%	No.	%
General fiction, all types	. . .	553	53	292	39
Scientific, technical, etc.	. . .	175	17	133	18
Practical, hobbies, sports	. . .	85	8	60	8
Literature, drama, poetry	. . .	69	7	40	5
Philosophy, religion, social sciences	. .	59	6	47	6
Travel	. . . . .	38	4	48	7
History, current affairs	. . . .	31	3	34	5
Art and the arts	. . . . .	17	2	22	3
Biography	. . . . .	8	1	36	5
Unclassifiable above	. . . .	10	1	22	3
Total books .	. . . . .	1045	100	734	100

fiction was so popular it is not surprising that 'just something to read' was the main category, and under a fifth of books borrowed were specific titles.

It cannot be assumed that when people borrow books

Table 36

Reason for Choice of Book

	No.	%
Specific title . . .	197	19
Specific subject . .	374	36
Just something to read .	474	45
Total books . . .	1045	100

from a library they are necessarily borrowing just for themselves. People who use five, six or seven tickets may be asumed to be using someone else's tickets besides their own since three tickets is the normal issue though a fourth ticket restricted to non-fiction can be requested. Of the books considered in the survey 87 per cent were being borrowed for the borrower's own use and the remaining 13 per cent were for other people. A similar question was asked by Marsterson[1] in a survey of a West Riding county branch library at Maltby, a town of 15,000 people in the centre of the South Yorkshire coalfield, and he found 23 per cent of the books being borrowed were for other people. This difference may reflect the greater range of books available at the Sheffield Central Library which provides many books for specialist interests, whereas the Maltby library is more of a local library to which people go for their general borrowing, so that the one visitor may be collecting books for several people.

In the Sheffield survey a further question was added to try to find out for whom books had been chosen in the case of the 13 per cent for other people. The majority of them (52%) were for the borrower's wife or husband, a further 18 per cent were for parents, another 17 per cent were for other relatives such as sons, daughters, aunts, uncles, etc., and a rather surprisingly large 14 per cent were for friends.

The final detailed analysis of the 1,045 books borrowed concerned the purpose for which they were being bor-

[1] W. Marsterson, 'The Library at Maltby: a Survey of the Adult Membership and Use of the County Branch Library at Maltby, West Riding'. Dissertation for M.A. in Librarianship, University of Sheffield, 1969.

rowed. Respondents were asked to say for each book whether it was being borrowed for (a) work (b) hobby or similar interest or (c) just leisure reading. A similar analysis was made by Marsterson in his Maltby study and so Table 37 gives comparative data for the two libraries. It is interesting to see how the Sheffield Central Library borrowings had 25 per cent of books borrowed for 'work' purposes, whilst this was only 6 per cent at Maltby, though in both cases the majority of books were being borrowed just for leisure reading. The differences in books borrowed for work purposes again reflects the different functions of the two libraries and draws attention to the importance of the large and varied non-fiction stock held by the central library of the city, and the problems for librarians of providing any similar facilities in the very much more widespread country areas.

Table 37

Purposes of Books Borrowed

	Sheffield		Maltby	
	No.	%	No.	%
For work . . .	260	25	45	6
For hobbies, etc. .	111	11	101	15
For leisure reading .	674	64	528	78
Total books . .	1045	100	674	100

Of course, people do not always find the books they are wanting when they visit a lending library and 156 people (21%) of the Sheffield borrowers said they had not found a particular book they had been looking for. Of 161 books named by these people 37 per cent were fiction titles, 17 per cent were technical or scientific and 16 per cent were books on hobbies and practical interests. But as Table 36 showed, 45 per cent of books borrowed were 'just to read', and the respondents were asked how they actually went about choosing books which were 'just to read'. Three hundred and five people were able to give an answer and 37 per cent said they looked for specific authors, 35 per cent said that they picked out covers that caught their eye (an interesting point since most books are shown spine outwards on the shelves), 14 per cent said that they had chosen a book in a subject they were interested in. This wide diversity of ways of choosing books 'just to read' does seem to indicate how borrowers can be helped by displays of books of all types arranged in the library by the staff. The Sheffield Central Library has two double-sided display stands which enables them to arrange four different special displays and it has three sets of shelves for 'recommended' fiction – though it is sometimes difficult to decide on what grounds the library staff decide a book shall go on these shelves.

Of course, the library has staff who are available at all times in the lending section to help borrowers, so the survey respondents were asked if they had consulted assistants about anything during their visit. Only 52 (10%) had done so, but their reasons were very varied as Table 38 shows. (Although the numbers are small the percentaging helps for comparison.) It may also be noted that, although the bases of calculation are not exactly the same, a third of the *books bought* at Ward's involved some

Table 38

Consulted Assistants in Library

	No.	%
For information about a book .	12	23
To find location of types of books	11	21
Queries about tickets . .	10	19
To reserve a book . . .	8	15
To ask about a book not in stock .	6	12
To join the library . . .	5	10
Total	52	100

help from an assistant and this would probably involve just under 15 per cent of all the actual *customers*.

In addition to the personal help obtainable from assistants there are also subject and author catalogues available for public use in the lending library. Eighty-six people (17%) used the catalogue during their visit, 57 per cent to look up a particular title, 28 per cent to look up books within a particular subject and 15 per cent to look up a particular author.

These two analyses show that, on the whole, people who visit the lending library make relatively little use of the catalogue or the library assistants. Of course, much of the borrowing is done for leisure or recreational purposes and borrowers do not want to do anything more than browse along the shelves. Indeed, it has surprised the present writer in talking to university students to find how many of them, in seeking books for essays or even dissertations, do not seem to do anything more than look along the shelves – catalogues and assistants rarely being used.

This section of the chapter has dealt with particular aspects of the visit to the library for which comparisons with the bookshop are not really possible. The next section gives some details for which bookshop comparisons are possible.

Library Visits with Bookshop Comparisons

In both surveys respondents were asked in what way their visit to the library or bookshop was a part of any other calls they were making in the town. Table 39 shows how the visit to the library was much more a 'special visit' than was the one to the bookshop, and more people called at the library on their way to or from work and school. This leaves the call which was 'part of other shopping', as the predominant category for the bookshop, which may be expected to predominate since Ward's bookshop is more in the shopping centre of the city than is the public library which is just a little distance away from the shops. This analysis is interesting in the light of discussions which are often held about the siting of libraries, particularly in new towns. Clearly if it were possible to site main libraries near to bookshops, and both of them in the shopping (rather than the civic) centres of the town it is likely that both would benefit.

It was very difficult to compare the sections of the library visited with those of the bookshop since the layouts of the two places are quite different. The lending library has its non-fiction classified by the Dewey decimal system, though biography is a special separate section. Fiction is, of course, quite separate as in most public libraries, and this was visited by easily the largest proportion of library users

Table 39
Reason for Visit

	Library		Ward's	
	No.	%	No.	%
A special visit	190	37	69	20
Part of other shopping	128	25	167	49
On way from or to work or school .	121	24	47	14
During lunch hour	52	10	29	9
Called in 'passing by' . . .	16	3	17	5
Other reasons	3	1	11	3
Total	510	100	340	100

though 46 per cent is still only a minority of people and is
slightly surprising. Table 40 gives what comparisons are
possible, percentages being based on the total number of
people which allows for people visiting several sections.

Table 40
Sections Visited

	Library		Ward's	
	No.	%	No.	%
Fiction.	237	46	{ 48a	14
			89	26
Hobbies, practical etc. . . .	60	12	32	26
Literature, languages and the arts . .	85	17	67	20
Social sciences	49	10	—	—
Science and technical . . .	47	9	57	17
Travel	45	9	46	13
Biography	39	8	14	4

(a) 'Paperbacks' here equated with fiction.

All the visitors to the library were asked how often they visited it, and, since 84 per cent of the visitors to Ward's bookshop said they were members of the public library the same question was put to them. Since books are loaned for two weeks one might expect a fairly general pattern of fortnightly borrowing and this was so for the great majority of people, with 83 per cent of the library users and 75 per cent of the bookshop customers visiting at least fortnightly. Only 7 per cent of the library users said they went to the library less than once a month in general. When the types of books *generally* borrowed by the two groups were compared fiction was, of course, the main category for both groups, though it was interesting to see that the Ward's customers claimed to do more borrowing of non-fiction books than did the library users, this perhaps

Table 41

Types of Books Generally Borrowed

	Library		Ward's	
	No.	%	No.	%
Fiction.	292	40	162	31
Scientific, technical, etc. . .	133	18	97	19
Hobbies, practical . . .	60	8	67	13
Travel	48	7	36	7
Socal sciences	47	6	0	—
Literature, drama, poetry . .	40	5	22	4
Biography	36	5	25	5
History, current affairs . .	34	5	45	9
Art and the arts	22	3	25	5
Unclassifiable above . . .	22	3	40	8
Total books	734	100	519	100

being a reflection of the large proportion of students among the Ward's customers.

The above tables have dealt with the borrowing habits of both the bookshop and library users. It is now the turn of book buying to be looked at for these two groups of people.

Book buying amongst Library Users and Bookshop Customers
We have already noted that only 4 per cent of the people who had visited Ward's bookshop said that they had not bought any books at all over the past year. The library users were asked, 'Do you ever buy books?' to which 22 per cent said that they did not. Table 42 gives a comparison of the numbers of books that the two groups of respondents claimed to have bought over the past year and shows clearly the greater amount of buying amongst the bookshop customers. (These figures do not include the charming interview given to an all unsuspecting interviewer who

Table 42

	Library		Ward's	
	No.	%	No.	%
None . . .	114	22	14	4
1–4	127	25	35	10
5–9	91	18	67	20
10–19. . .	69	14	92	27
20 and over . .	98	19	132	39
No answer . .	11	2	0	—
Total . . .	510	100	340	100

approached the proprietor himself, Mr A. B. Ward, and was very baffled indeed when he claimed to have bought several thousands of books over the year!)

Even though the bookshop customers were greater book buyers than the library users, as might have been expected, the book buying habits of the library users are important. Those who did buy were all asked what sort of books they bought so that these results could be compared with the types of books usually bought by bookshop customers. There were the usual sorts of books mentioned in the replies of respondents, but it was interesting to see that 72 per cent of library users mentioned non-fiction categories compared with 65 per cent of the bookshop customers. A further point of interest was that a quarter of the library users specifically mentioned the purchase of paperback books.

Since giving and receiving books as gifts is an important aspect of books it was felt that it would be useful to see how much the library users and the bookshop customers were involved in these activities. Tables 43 and 44 give the details and comparisons. It can be seen that both giving and receiving books is more common amongst the bookshop customers and they tend to give a little more fiction and a little less non-fiction than the library users. They also give more to friends and relations, whereas library users tend to give more to children. The bookshop customers receive slightly more fiction than the library users, but they receive a great deal more non-fiction than them. Their gifts come more from relations and less from friends compared with the library people.

Table 43
Giving Books

	Library		Ward's	
	No.	%	No.	%
Do give . . .	282	55	249	73
Do not give . .	228	45	91	27
Total . . .	510	100	340	100
Give fiction . .	44	16	46	19
Give non-fiction . .	49	17	29	12
Give children's . .	73	26	52	21
Give to friends . .	125	44	138	55
Give to relatives . .	69	24	122	49
Give to children .	87	31	34	14

Note:—In the above table and the one below the 'give' and 'receive' percentages are examples of main categories based on the total numbers of people who do give or receive.

Table 44
Receiving Books

	Library		Ward's	
	No.	%	No.	%
Do receive . . .	226	44	232	68
Do not receive . .	284	56	108	32
Total . . .	510	100	340	100
Receive fiction . .	45	20	55	24
Receive non-fiction .	87	38	156	67
Receive from friends .	120	53	83	36
Receive from relatives .	104	46	151	65

The questions and answers dealt with in this section have been mainly concerned with the buying habits of bookshop customers and library borrowers. In the next and final analysis section details are given of the respondents' involvement in the world of books. Questions deal with when people began to borrow and buy books, how much their friends and families borrow and buy and what sort of people the respondents associate with bookshops and libraries.

Borrowing, Buying and the World of Books
It has been stressed in this and other books on reading that it is important for people to become used to books at an early age, so either the people in the two surveys were asked when they began using the public library or when they began to buy books. As Table 45 shows, both activities began fairly early in life and it would seem, not unnaturally, that the borrowing habit was established

Table 45

When Began to Borrow and Buy Books

	Library (Borrowing)		Ward's (Buying)	
	No.	%	No.	%
At primary school .	255	50	100	29
At secondary school .	88	17	131	39
At college . .	12	2	36	11
After leaving school .	13	3	33	10
Could not be sure .	142	28	40	12
Total . . .	510	100	340	100

before the buying one, though for most of the book buyers the period at school was the time when they began to buy. Unfortunately this table's value is reduced by the large proportions of people who could not remember clearly and answers such as 'A long time ago' or 'Just at school' could not be satisfactorily classified.

Clearly most people who borrow and buy books are to some degree involved in what may be called 'book culture' – a way of life in which books play a part in people's lives for work, hobbies and leisure. It would be surprising if the people whose lives include enjoying books did not have friends and relations who also were used to having books in their lives, so questions about these people were asked in the two surveys. For the borrowers questions were asked about the borrowing habits of their friends and near relations, for the buyers similar questions

Table 46

Borrowing and Buying: Friends

	Library (Borrowing)		Ward's (Buying)	
	No.	%	No.	%
Most friends . .	294	58	181	53
Some friends . .	82	16	59	17
A few friends . .	88	17	53	16
None . .	24	5	29	9
No answer . .	22	4	18	5
Total . . .	510	100	340	100

were asked about the buying habits of their friends and relations.

Table 46 shows that for 58 per cent of the borrowers 'most' of their friends were library users too, whilst for 53 per cent of the buyers 'most' of their friends bought books and only 9 per cent said that 'none' of their friends were buyers.

Each respondent was asked if he had, living, a father or mother and a husband or wife; then for those people who had such living relatives they were asked to what degree they borrowed books in the case of the library sample and bought books in the case of the bookshop sample. Standard pre-set responses of often/sometimes/rarely/never were used for all the replies. The replies showed considerable similarity in borrowing habits, with just about two-thirds of all fathers, mothers and spouses being in the 'often' category for borrowing. But for the buying of the bookshop customers' relatives only a minority bought 'often', with spouses being in the lead with 25 per cent. Of course, buying is bound to be at a lower rate than borrowing, but the 37 per cent of fathers and 40 per cent of mothers who were said 'never' to buy books is a striking point and may be interpreted pessimistically as denoting an older generation of non-buyers or optimistically as showing a new generation who are greater buyers of books. For ease of reading the details of borrowing and buying are separated into two tables.

It was felt that the library users might have some image in their minds of the sort of people who use libraries, and similarly that bookshop users might have some stereotype of bookshop customers. So to both groups a question was

Table 47

Borrowing of Library Users' Relatives

				Father		Mother		Spouse	
				No.	%	No.	%	No.	%
Often	.	.	.	93	65	105	67	117	71
Sometimes	.	.	.	31	22	31	20	33	20
Rarely	.	.	.	16	11	16	10	13	8
Never	.	.	.	2	1	4	3	1	1
Total	.	.	.	142	100	156	100	164	100

Table 48

Buying of Bookshop Users' Relatives

				Father		Mother		Spouse	
				No.	%	No.	%	No.	%
Often	.	.	.	33	17	25	12	33	25
Sometimes	.	.	.	48	24	54	26	41	32
Rarely	.	.	.	46	23	48	23	39	30
Never	.	.	.	73	37	84	40	17	13
Total	.	.	.	200	100	211	100	130	100

put asking them if they associated libraries (or bookshops)
with particular kinds of people. The interviewers were not
allowed to make any helpful suggestions in putting these
questions so, not surprisingly, a lot of respondents found
them rather too difficult to answer. But of the people who

did reply it was interesting to note that 18 per cent of library users said they associated libraries with 'all types' of people, whilst 8 per cent each mentioned 'students' or 'intellectuals'. For the bookshop users 14 per cent mentioned 'students' and 7 per cent 'intellectuals'. The results are small, but they do indicate a higher level of social status expectation in the bookshop.

Table 49

People Associated with Libraries/Bookshops

	Library (library)		Ward's (bookshop)	
	No.	%	No.	%
No particular kind of person . . .	272	54	205	60
All types of people	93	18	—	—
Students	41	8	49	14
Intellectuals	41	8	25	7
Better class, middle class . . .	11	2	17	5
Well-educated, cultured . . .	15	3	—	—
Self-improvers	17	3	—	—
People with plenty of time . .	17	3	—	—

Note:—As people could give more than one suggestion percentages are not totalled as they could exceed 100%.

Conclusions

This chapter has ranged widely over a large number of questions put to library users and in many cases has given comparisons with similar questions about bookshops.

The library users represent a broader social cross-section of the general public than the bookshop customers, but even though the library attracts more people from the lower ranks of the managerial and supervisory types of occupations and also from the higher manual occupations of a technical and supervisory type it still does not get very far with the bulk of the ordinary manual occupations. This means that the library users, whilst not so middle class in occupations and with lower educational backgrounds than the bookshop users, are still a cut above the general population. The library users contain a good proportion of young people, and about two out of five borrowers are under twenty-five years of age, but again the bookshop customers have even more young people and these young people are more often in higher education, particularly at university. So the library users are older, of lower social status and educational attainment than the bookshop customers. But this is a very high-level comparison, and compared with the *general* population the library users are of higher social status and educational attainment.

The use made of the lending library is clearly of a varied sort, with fiction reading for pure leisure playing a very important part. In choosing fiction 'just to read' the author's name is important as are the covers and their blurbs. One has only to watch people in the fiction stocks of any public library to see how people work their way along the shelves, picking out books here and there as they go along. It would therefore seem useful to develop ways of helping people to extend their fictional interests and the rather hackneyed shelf of 'recommended novels' hardly does this since they appear frequently to be just the 'safe' names. Sheffield City Libraries do publish lists of names of writers to help readers try out new authors, but it might be interesting if experiments could be carried out to try to link types of writers together so that a person who enjoys books by X could go to a small catalogue and looks up a set of names suggested by the library staff along the lines that 'if you enjoy reading X's books then you may well enjoy reading P, Q, R and S as well'. Since P's list would probably contain some names not on X's list the reader could then gradually extend his field of fiction reading helped along by the card index. A further possible way of helping the fiction searchers would be to pin up reviews from the Sunday papers once the new fiction was on the shelves. This would certainly help those many people who mean to look for a book which caught their eye in the review columns, but whose name and author they have forgotten by the time the book has been bought, classified, catalogued, read by the library staff and has eventually found its way on to the fiction shelves.

But by no means all the library borrowing is just for recreational fiction, and it is clear that the borrowers also use the lending library a good deal for their work and for their hobbies. Over a third of borrowing is concerned with these interests and many of them lie in the non-fiction categories of the library. The Sheffield library has its non-fiction (apart from biography) well set out on a system of continuous shelves which follow the Dewey classification system and the sections are clearly labelled to help the reader. Perhaps the fact that only 17 per cent of borrowers used the catalogues at all indicates that for many purposes a look along the shelf is sufficient for most people's needs. Nevertheless it is clear that the library user who is at home with the classification system can use it more efficiently and here it is clear that many young people receive precious little instruction in library usage. The rather dreary visits to the library when too many children have to be shown too much in too little time are not the answer to this problem. Rather the emphasis, as in most modern education, should be on getting the children involved in *using* a properly classified library at school so that they *personally* learn the value, and even the enjoyment, of being able to add to their knowledge by the proper use of books. The writer's own experience with schoolchildren and university students seems to indicate that very few children receive adequate instruction in the use of libraries at school and it is disheartening and frustrating to set essay work for social science students at university who are clearly ill prepared to use a large and well-stocked academic library.

All this adds up to the point that the surveys show the library users to be some way towards involvement in the world of books, but, on the whole, not as greatly involved as the people who use the bookshop. The library borrowers *do* buy books – at least 78 per cent of them claimed to do so – but their buying is at a much lesser rate than that of the bookshop customers. The borrowers also give and receive books as presents, but again at a lesser rate than the book buyers. But one cannot but feel that the book borrowers and the book buyers overlap to a considerable extent and the functions of the bookshop and library, whilst being different, are in many ways complementary. The borrower may use the library as a place to look at books, to sample them and to use them on a temporary basis. The bookshop, usually on a smaller scale but with the advantage of having so much *new* stock, is again a place of display, for looking at books and then for acquiring them permanently. It does seem clear that the borrowers must be encouraged to want to own books by the act of borrowing, and the book buyers are often encouraged to buy after having borrowed from the public library. Perhaps the book buyers may be said to have got that much further into the culture of books, but certainly the ranks of the borrowers appear to contain many likely recruits.

Chapter 5

Light Fiction and the Romantic Novel

Introduction

The extreme right-hand end of the theoretical model of book reading deals with leisure reading which may be categorised as reading for distraction rather than for self-improvement or work. In this type of reading we suggest that the reader is gaining intrinsic satisfaction as the book is being read purely for the pleasure it gives at the time of reading, and not (as may be the case with 'social' reading) for the status it confers on the reader for having read it or for the 'external' reason that the reader feels that the book is of some literary importance and should therefore be read to extend his literary knowledge. Distraction reading is, therefore, a largely personal matter which may give pleasure to the reader at the time of reading, but which has little 'carry-over' beyond the act of reading. Having read a book in this category we do not feel that anything of great mental significance has happened – we might even feel that we could just as well have watched a television programme, gone to the cinema or pub, or indulged in any of a dozen other forms of leisure activity which can fill in our leisure time. It is clear then that distraction reading can be considered from a number of viewpoints. In one sense it can be analysed from an individual point of view to consider what happens to the person who reads the book; what mental or psychological processes occur in this activity? In another way this type of reading can be looked at more socially to consider the various factors which may explain why such books and readers do exist. After all, it is known that many titles in light fiction sell in great numbers, light novel authors are household names, yet this is a section of writing and reading which is rarely discussed in the literary or even sociological field. Why do we ignore this quantitatively important part of the book and reading world? Clearly there must be social forces operating which result in this lack of public attention being paid to what is a considerable field of writing, publishing and reading.

Also, it is important in any analysis of individual or social activities to see what light can be shed by placing the problem in an historical context. What is happening today can often be seen more clearly, if not necessarily 'explained', by considering what has happened in the past. We shall therefore try to set modern light reading in an historical context as well as the contemporary one.

Quantitative data on the reading of light fiction is difficult, if not impossible, to obtain for a number of reasons. Firstly the sales of titles are not recorded in any systematic way for any publication to which the 'public' have access. Clearly publishers do know what their sales are of each title, but equally they are not unnaturally reticent about telling the world, and therefore their rivals, how badly a particular book has sold. For this simple reason the public tends to learn about the best seller and particularly the 'block-buster' which sells in millions, but very little is said about the many other books which do moderately well or even fail to pay their way. A further problem when looking at the field of light literature is that it has hardly been investigated systematically at all in a historical sense. What writing there is about nineteenth-century light novels tends to look at them from one to two viewpoints. There is the very 'literary' point of view which deems them barely worthy of consideration because they are judged by the same criteria as 'serious' literature. Alternatively they are seen in the context of the development of 'working-class' reading and tend to be judged from a very value-laden viewpoint which frequently uses them as awful examples of how the newly literate wasted their time and energy. Neither of these perspectives are of much help to the sociologist who is trying to look at this aspect of literature objectively and wishing to understand the satisfactions derived from such reading without 'judging' it either literally or socially.

The avoidance of any serious discussion of light literature is in itself a most interesting social phenomenon. In these days which we are constantly being told are so permissive, people who are happy to talk about obscenity and pornography, and who quite openly espouse its dissemination, seem to be embarrassed by suggestions of disseminating simple romantic novels of impeccable moral purity. This itself is an interesting social situation which is not easy to explain, but the present situation is clearly a product of historical social changes and it is to the nineteenth century we now turn for an albeit brief consideration of light literature in the time when this country was becoming both literate and technically able to produce cheap books.

A Historical Perspective

In his fascinating study of 'The English Common Reader' between 1800 and 1900 Richard Altick[1] points out that in the first half of the nineteenth century politicians frequently feared the effects of an increasingly literate population, and the particular fear of 'demagogue-inspired rebellion' was often in their minds. It was only when fears of revolution diminished, at about the end of the fifties, that the more liberal-minded politicians began to see the working classes as potential allies and then their worries about reading and political activity began to decline. But when people worried less about political repercussions from reading they began to worry more about the possibilities of moral corruption. The early nineteenth century was a time of great concern about the effects of industrialisation and increasing urbanisation, as is exemplified by the founding in 1802 of the Society for the Suppression of Vice and the Encouragement of Religion and Virtue. A great deal of leisure time was undoubtedly spent on the traditional British pastimes of drinking, gambling and whoring, and Sunday observance was always in peril. In the development of reading various associations were active, and Altick claims that 'The Society for Pure Literature was as characteristic of the sixties as the Society for the Diffusion of Useful Knowledge had been in the thirties.' Clearly the middle years of the century were years of uncertainty for many people who thought about the effects of spreading literacy.

In 1852 it is claimed that *Uncle Tom's Cabin* sold 150,000

[1] Richard Altick, *The English Common Reader*, 1800–1900, University of Chicago Press, Chicago, 1957.

copies in six months. This was also the period of the growth of the great system of local public lending libraries such as Mudie's in 1842 and Smith's in 1852. But whilst the middle-class *Punch* began in 1841, the working-class *Titbits* did not arrive until 1881. For all the spread of books and newspapers and magazines (the two latter helped by exemption from tax from 1861) the quality of the products never ceased to give concern. Literary and social commentators seriously questioned whether the reading habit which so many people appeared to be acquiring was necessarily a good habit. More people than before were reading, but were they reading the 'right' things for the 'right' reasons? Chambers admitted in 1840 that his 'Penny Magazine' was read only by the élite of the labouring community, but this magazine and the earlier Chambers Journal gave rise to many cheaper and tawdrier imitations which were often short-lived but nevertheless attracted many readers during their lives.

In the world of books the 'novel' from the 'circulating library' had been suspect reading for many years and even in 1775 Sir Anthony Absolute had warned Mrs Malaprop of its dangers to women. 'Madam, a circulating library in a town is as an evergreen tree of diabolical knowledge! It blossoms through the year! – and depend on it, Mrs Malaprop, that they who are so fond of handling the leaves will long for the fruit at last.' Even late in the nineteenth century Matthew Arnold inveighed against the lending libraries for being 'a machinery for the multiplication and protection of bad literature, and for keeping good books dear.' And he added that 'The three shilling book is our great want . . . [not] a cheap literature, hideous and ignoble of aspect, like the tawdry novels which flare on the book-shelves of our railway stations.'

The nineteenth century was clearly a time when increase in quantity appeared to raise great doubts about the direction of quality. The medium was expanding and was clearly, in itself, a desirable thing, but the message for which it was being used worried those people who felt themselves to be the responsible members of society. Many of the parallels with social reaction to television are quite close, though television, because of the close quasi-governmental control over it, has never as yet had much of a problem of obscenity or pornography.

The end of the nineteenth century saw a society developing in which the ability to read was rapidly becoming the birth-right of every citizen, and the new literacy was ably responded to in newspapers and maga-zines by such people as Newne with *Titbits* and Harms-worth, whose *Daily Mail* of 1896 was the first mass circulation popular daily paper. Clearly reading was popular, though with every development of society book reading had to meet new competition. It is not always recognised by the more literary-minded historians that book reading as a leisure activity in the nineteenth century had to compete more and more with other forms of leisure activity. Altick notes that particularly between 1860 and 1890 'the three requisites of a mass reading public – literacy, leisure and a little pocket money – became the possession of more and more people.' Clearly this was so, but leisure was being catered for by many other activities besides books. Newspapers and magazines provided ample reading matter for many people and more affluent clerical and skilled manual workers had the choice of thriving theatres (and later cinemas) for their evenings. Excursions and holidays grew tremendously, with the growth of the railways and, for individual travel, with the bicycle and the motor car. Sport boomed in the latter half of the century and by the twentieth century organised sport was established in many previously unorganised sectors. The FA Cup Final which attracted an audience of 4,000 in 1880 had 110,000 spectators in 1901. All these activities, which competed for the time of people, have to be seen as growing at the same time as literacy and books. With hours of work still very long for the employed people and the sixty-hour week with Saturday afternoon off *common* amongst workers in the 1860s and 70s, leisure time was still restricted. And it should not be overlooked that surveys by Booth and Rowntree at the turn of the century still found 10 per cent of the population in dire poverty and a further 20 per cent so close to it as never to be safe. For many people in the early twentieth century, life still offered little in the way of 'literacy, leisure and a little pocket money'. The mass of the British working class was still too near the margin of subsistence to be closely associated with 'literature'. Public libraries spread in the twentieth century, with lendings increasing each year, but it was only in 1938 that Allen Lane produced his first revolutionary 'paperback' Penguin, and so the world of the really cheap book of good quality is barely thirty years old. This is not to say that the Penguin was the first cheap book; there were thousands and millions of these before then, but the inception of the Penguin series is now generally regarded as the point in time where quantity and quality got back together again. Before then the two had been too far divorced.

After the 1939–45 war the growth of publishing was hampered by shortages of all kinds, but the popular paperback gradually developed and in the early 1960s there was a growth which is now sometimes called the 'paperback revolution'. Certainly today the bookshops, department stores, newsagents, station bookstalls and a host of other 'outlets' are stacked high with cheap books and the range of choice is enormous. In conventional 'serious' bookshops academic and literary paperbacks share place with 'popular' novels. In newsagents and other such outlets light paperbacks compete with magazines. The paperbacks of Corgi, Pan, Panther, Fontana, Mayflower, Four-Square, and so on, all with their pictorial, gaily-coloured covers offer themselves for the people's leisure consumption. Sales can be very high indeed for popular authors. It is claimed that Victoria Holt's first three books sold 600,000 copies. Micky Spillane is advertised as the world's best-selling author, and his 'detective' Mike Hammer is a well-known figure. Popular authors sell in the hundreds of thousands, and books which are heavily publicised, such as *Valley of the Dolls*, may sell in millions.

Yet little has ever been published about the readers of light-fiction books, and if publishers are to be believed (and now and then they can be), practically no research has been carried out on paperback readers. Even the commercial subscription-survey of paperback books started by Opinion Research Centre was greeted by a public expression of doubts as to its usefulness. For the publisher the flair and the mystique are still enough for adequate profits, but for the sociologist they provide little to work on. We must therefore turn to other sources and these are scant.

The Modern Situation

The popularity of modern light fiction is amply illustrated by the large numbers of copies of titles sold. Denise Robins, who is published by Hodder and Stoughton, is said to sell nearly 300,000 copies a year in paperback. By mid-1969 Len Deighton's book *An Expensive Place to Die* was said to have sold over 400,000 copies. These two authors exemplify the two main categories of mass-consumption popular fiction. For the female reader there is the conventional romance story which has changed relatively little over a period of decades. For the male there is the more modern 'thriller' which is now epitomised by Ian Fleming's books which had James Bond as their central character. In this type of masculine story there is a mixture of adventure, sex, violence and mystery. In some cases the central male character is a spy or government agent of one sort or another, in other cases he is a detective (often a private one), but what is common, whatever the occupation may be, is a series of happenings which by convention include promiscuous sexual behaviour and illegal physical assaults, up to and including murder. The contrast between the male thriller and the female romance in their basic moral assumptions is quite striking. Of course, there are other types of light fiction, often of a traditional type such as the 'Western' which has a small but devoted band of readers, and the conventional 'detective' story in which the interest lies in unravelling a problem related to crime and (increasingly with the Simenon type of approach) dealing with the personalities of the people involved. A further type of fiction which has developed almost a cult-like support is science fiction. Here there is a relatively recent development from what in pre-war days was often called 'pulp-magazine' writing to a level of literature which is now seriously reviewed and discussed as a literary form.

Clearly, therefore, 'light' fiction is a category which, whilst it may be classed as one section of our theoretical continuum, is in fact a somewhat heterogeneous collection of different sorts of books written for different sorts of readers, and itself forming a continuum from the 'near-literature' to the lightest of the light distraction. The danger of this theoretical approach is that the continuum frequently becomes, not just a contrasting mechanism, but rather an evaluative one. With no difficulty at all 'popular' fiction is ranked lower than 'literary' fiction because it is judged by the canons of literary criticism applied to the more 'serious' type of writing. As a result of this one finds few successful analyses of light fiction made by literary critics. Hoggart[1] writes 'Some critics have also, in the last thirty years, been unwilling to try to analyse the social and moral significance not just of 'high literature' but of 'low' literature or mass literature ... Here one thinks again, for instance of *Scrutiny*, of Mrs Leavis's *Fiction and the Reading Public*[2] and of a few brilliant essays by George Orwell.'

[1] Richard Hoggart, *Contemporary Cultural Studies*, Occasional Papers No. 6, March 1969, Centre for Contemporary Cultural Studies, Birmingham University.
[2] Queenie Leavis, *Fiction and the Reading Public*, Chatto & Windus, London, 1932.

But such writers, and particularly the Leavises, are extremely literary people and it is open to question whether their viewpoints on mass literature are appropriate. Queenie Leavis's book begins by claiming to be objective but rapidly becomes a polemic against 'popular' literature in which such authors as Rudyard Kipling, Arnold Bennett and Gilbert Frankau all come under her lash. This type of criticism arises from assessing one form of writing by criteria which are inappropriate to it. It is similar in many ways to the theatrical critic who castigates a D'Oyly Carte opera for its lack of social realism or who wishes to report the Black and White Minstrel Show to the Race Relations Board. The criteria are wrong; the same critic does not castigate Royal Court experimental productions for their lack of charm or absence of story-line. One might just as well compare a conventional strip-joint exhibition with Tynan's serious intellectual venture into erotica with *Oh! Calcutta!*

Clearly what is fairer is an analysis of the social functions of light literature so that the books can be socially as well as literally evaluated. Then more realistic criteria of success can be set down, and it may well be that light literature can be considered in a more relevant way and also can be viewed more sympathetically, which at present is so rarely the case.

The Functions of Light Literature

Light literature is essentially leisure reading and as such can be studied in a number of theoretical ways. For example, leisure time can be used for purposes of self-improvement and personality development; it can equally be used for simple relaxation and rest. Most light literature caters explicitly for the latter. Leisure time can also be used to extend one's interests in the working day or it can be used for developing quite distinctly different interests. The former way can be exemplified by a person in a particular job who reads in his leisure time about that job because it interests him so much; in professional occupations such 'leisure' reading may be difficult to distinguish from 'work' reading because the reader himself makes little distinction in his time between work and leisure. On the other hand reading, and particularly light reading, can compensate the person who has a dull and uninteresting job. The spy thriller offers a vicarious world of experience to the man in the humdrum job, especially if he has a dull leisure life too. It has been suggested that women's romances cater for the young girl who yearns for a fairy-tale wooing but is rather young for it, and also for the aged spinster who yearns for such a wooing but, sadly, is past it. For both sexes this leisure reading is vicarious and compensatory.

Light modern fiction is best seen in a context of provision for leisure and it must therefore be seen as being in competition with other forms of leisure. In regarding it in this way in the nineteenth century it may be noted that the later part of that century was a time of developing sporting interests, and shortly after this in the early twentieth century the cinema began its tremendous development. Today we have television replacing the cinema as the great time-consuming activity, and for many people twenty hours before the television set a week is average viewing. It could therefore be argued that the leisure function of reading has been largely pushed out in the evenings by the television programme. Yet this is so only at a superficial level of 'consuming time'. To equate television viewing with reading is to ignore the difference between the two forms of media – the pictorial screen and the written word. Television viewing, often done in group form in the family living room, is a passive form of leisure activity which can be shared between people. Indeed, when the television set dominates the only living-room the sharing of the experience may be reluctantly accepted by the unwilling viewer who has nowhere else to go, except out of the home or to bed. Reading, by contrast, is an active form of leisure pursuit which requires the reader to undertake the positive activity of deciphering the written word and creating his own mental images. No matter how trivial or simple the content matter of a book may be the reader is 'engaged' with the book. Frequently readers are 'lost to the world' in a way which is rarely found with television viewing. At times the television viewer may appear hypnotised by the flickering screen, but this, again, is a passive sort of hypnosis and not a separateness which can be truly compared with that arising from reading. The reader is, from his act of reading, constructing a world of his own; the television viewer is merely receiving a world which has been created for him and several million other people. Some people react against television productions based on books for reasons closely connected with these points. Probably all of us at some time or other have seen a television show, or even a film in the cinema, based on a literary figure and have not enjoyed the show because the character from the book was 'wrong'. This can even occur on radio when a character's voice is 'wrong'; I myself can recall hearing a Dorothy L. Sayer's play where Lord Peter Wimsey was quite 'wrong' because the actor's voice did not 'fit' the mental voice which I had always associated with Lord Peter. Similarly in the recent television production of *Vanity Fair* I know of one person who would not watch it because Susan Hampshire did not 'fit' Becky Sharp. These examples demonstrate the essentially *personal* way in which the book reader is able to create his or her own personal images of faces, voices and so on in the process of reading. This involvement between author and reader is, we submit, quite unique to the printed word, and occurs particularly in vicarious leisure reading, especially where the reader identifies with the hero or heroine.

Much leisure reading is done in the evenings and at weekends when the reader is in a relaxed frame of mind, and there are strong indications from informal questioning of young people that reading in bed is a particularly successful setting for 'getting away' from the world of reality. We have no systematic data on bedtime reading, but impressions suggest that the fact of being in bed (especially for young unmarried people) enhances the 'privateness' of the reading activity and makes the escape from reality more easy.

In the light novel itself it is accepted that the skilful author is one who can quickly engage the attention of the reader. The light novel is essentially simple in its form and has quickly identifiable principal characters. Often these main people are almost stereotypes of heroes, heroines, villains, servants and so on and their very lack of complexity helps the reader understand the story quickly. This 'ease of entry' to the book is useful for the less-skilled reader who is not 'put-off' and it is acceptable also to the more highly skilled reader who accepts the convention in *this* form of reading, though he would scorn it in a more 'literary' form of fiction.

It is, therefore, incorrect reasoning to suggest, as one public librarian has done, that 'on the whole less of the lightest kind of novels are now being provided by public libraries as the need for that kind of entertainment is increasingly being met by television.' We submit that the needs met by books are not the same as those met by television except in the simplest sense of time-filling leisure activity.

Light Romantic Fiction

In the period of the present research it has not been possible to carry out any systematic research into the readership of male modern fiction, though this has been discussed in general interviews where appropriate. It has, however, been possible to carry out a survey of some women who are relatively enthusiastic readers of romantic novels, and this section gives details of this survey.

In the first year of the research I met (for other reasons than an interest in romances) Mr John Boon, the managing director of Mills & Boon, and was able to carry out an empirical enquiry in this field. In a very general discussion with Mr Boon I learned that Mills & Boon have a mailing list of about 9,000 people who, twice a year, receive a pamphlet about the forthcoming half-year's romance publications. Mills & Boon, when the research began in

1967, were publishing between 7 and 12 titles in hard-covers and 6 paperbacks each month; the paperbacks have now been increased to 8 a month. There is of course considerable overlap between the hardcover and paper-back titles, most of the paperbacks having been published originally in hardcovers some months before. The mailing list is drawn up simply from letters received from readers of the romances. Each Mills & Boon romance which falls a few pages short of the conventional 192 pages (a size which derives from standard sheets of paper) carries adver-tisements of forthcoming titles for the next few months. Sometimes readers are invited to write to Mills & Boon if they wish to be kept informed of forthcoming titles. Each person who is put on the mailing list has therefore shown enough initiative actually to write a letter of request; there is no simple addressed, postage pre-paid postcard inserted in the book. After two years recipients of the catalogues are asked to say if they wish to remain on the mailing list and again a positive reply is requested. These points are stressed simply because it is important to note that in using the mailing list as a sample of romance readers the sampling is of a quite definite type of reader – one who is undoubtedly a romance *aficionado*. Neverthe-less the existence of such a mailing list seemed to have great possibilities for a questionnaire survey, and Mills & Boon kindly offered not only to send out a questionnaire with the 1968 Spring list, but also to bear all the costs of printing the questionnaire, return postage and analysis of results. This very generous offer made possible a study which our limited research resources could not have met.

The questionnaire itself was printed on a double sheet

of $11\frac{1}{2}$ x $6\frac{1}{2}$ in. paper and asked a number of questions about the reader herself (there were only two men on the list) her age, education, occupation, marital status, family and so on; there were then specific questions about her interest in Mills & Boon romances and further questions about her general leisure interests. An envelope, addressed to Mills & Boon with a pre-paid reply postage label, was attached and the usual small booklet describing forthcoming romance titles had a short 'editorial' asking the recipients to help in the survey. It must be made clear now that this survey was very much an experiment from which very poor results could have resulted. Knowing nothing about the mailing list recipients except their addresses there was no guide as to whether they were likely to reply, but it was recognised that many readers might well find a questionnaire rather beyond their literary skills, and the surveyor was aware that a postal questionnaire was inferior to interviews for this sort of sample. But interviews all over the country were out of the question for reasons of both cost and time, and it was finally agreed by everyone that given reasonable replies at least *something* would be known about this field of reading.

Nearly 3,000 questionnaires were returned and 2,788 were coded and put on to punch cards for analysis. The response rate of about a third was proportionately rather low though numerically quite high. Many postal questionnaire surveys suffer from low response rates and one problem which then arises is to decide how representative the respondents are of the total group surveyed. One cannot know how the 3,000 respondents differ from those who did not reply, but one can, from previous survey experience, guess that the respondents are likely to be keener readers than the non-respondents, and one can guess that younger and more literate women would find completing a questionnaire easier than would older and less literate ones. A bias is expected in the response, therefore, towards the keener, the younger and the more literate readers. But it was noted in reading the returned questionnaires that some women who were quite old (even in their eighties) and some who were not very literate at all had clearly done their very best to complete the questionnaire because they wanted to help Mills & Boon.

The survey results gave a fairly 'flat' age distribution, with proportions above the national average in the age groups between 25 and 54, as Table 50 shows. Even allowing for bias in the response, this age distribution does show that the readers are not by any means just young girls and old maids.

Table 50

Age Groups	Per cent	National figures for women age 15 and over, 1966
Under 15	1	—
15–18	6 } 16	} 18
19–24	10	
25–34	21	15
35–44	21	16
45–54	17	16
55–65	12	16
65–74	8	12
75 and over	4	7
Total	100	100
N =	2,744	

On analysing marital status it was found that 55 per cent of respondents (compared to a national figure of 57 per cent) were married, 34 per cent were single, 10 per cent widowed and 1 per cent divorced. This shows a considerable variety of women reading romances – with the spinsters of any age accounting for only one-third. Furthermore, 45 per cent of the women had children of various ages at home, and a third of all the respondents were mothers with children under the age of 15. These, clearly, are not the frustrated spinsters of the conventional stereotype of romance readers. In fact 55 per cent of the respondents were now full-time housewives and of the occupations which the women were now in (or had been in before becoming housewives) over a third were clerical and secretarial jobs and over 10 per cent were technical or professional. The proportions with shop or factory jobs were under 20 per cent all together. It may well be, therefore, that the full-length 200 page, 70,000 word romantic novel is still beyond the literary capacity of many less able readers. The educational backgrounds of the respondents showed just below half having completed their education at an elementary or secondary school, whilst 17 per cent had been to technical, art or secretarial college and 6 per cent had been to a teacher training college or university. This last group may be considered by some to be 'above' the romantic novel by virtue of their higher education, but the *function* of the romance for women of this type is exemplified by the graduate computer programmer who said that she found the romances excellent relaxation after her day's work. Several women who ran businesses of their own expressed similar views.

The respondents were asked about their other leisure and reading interests. Seven per cent of respondents did not read a daily paper and 12 per cent did not read a Sunday paper; both of these are rather high figures for non-reading. Quite a lot of women read only their local papers and the papers which were more popular with them than national readership surveys figures show for all women readers were the *Daily Express, Daily Mail, Sunday Express, Sunday Times* and *Sunday Telegraph*. The *Daily* and *Sunday Mirrors* were below national figures, as were the *Sun, Guardian, People* and, particularly, the *News of the World*. This reading shows a very mixed bag, but clearly indicates that the respondents' newspaper choices were quite catholic. Television viewing was a 'frequent' activity for 30 per cent of the women, but 29 per cent said they viewed 'not very much' or 'never', which seems quite a high proportion. The type of programme most enjoyed was mainly a serial (usually BBC) or a film – both of which indicate enjoyment of a story. Cinema attendance was low, with 80 per cent going 'not very much' or 'never', but amongst those who did go the favourite actors and actresses were usually British 'straight' actors and actresses, again suggesting a liking for a story.

Nearly half the respondents claimed that they bought most (in some cases all) of the Mills & Boon paperback romances, though for the hardback editions this was only 4 per cent. An analysis of how many the respondents claimed to have bought in the past year showed 30 per cent claiming to have bought an average of three or more each month. This buying pattern is seen in extreme form in some written-in comments. One woman said that her husband had had to build two cupboards to store her collection of over 500. Another young housewife under 24 years old and with a son 16 months old wrote, 'They are marvellous except when you are a housewife and mother. 3s. 6d. is a lot out of your wages. But I go without a pair of nylons to get the books.'

The romances are bought at a wide variety of retail outlets with conventional bookshops, W. H. Smith's branches and Boots' branches prominent. A notable 17 per cent said they bought by post (at an extra 6d. per book) from 'Jane Lovell' who is a direct mail bookseller specialising in the Mills & Boon books and giving a very rapid and reliable service. Two-thirds of the readers borrowed Mills & Boon romances from public libraries, and (even though they have declined in number) commercial libraries still supply the romances to 19 per cent of readers.

It was clear that a great deal of borrowing and lending went on. Nearly a third of the readers had difficulty in satisfying their wants at public libraries either because stocks were low or demand was very high. Three-quarters of the women lent personal copies to other people and 46 per cent of respondents claimed to re-read the novels 'very often'. Perhaps the high usage of the books can best be exemplified by one account written on a questionnaire. 'After I have read the books my mother reads them, followed in turn by my aunt, who returns them to me. They are then passed on to a neighbour who is a pensioner and widow – she in turn reads them, and they are then taken to a home for elderly and infirm ladies. I feel you will appreciate that your books bring considerable pleasure to many people, particularly in view of the fact that the ladies at the home, so I am told, look forward to the lady taking them in to them.'

Of course, some of the respondents had been romance readers for many years and over a quarter claimed to have been readers for 20 years or more. But 42 per cent had been readers under 10 years and 25 per cent had been readers less than 5 years. This spread, like that of the age distribution, shows that there is clearly a new generation of readers as well as an older one. This means that Mills & Boon romantic novels are catering for, and apparently giving satisfaction to, a more heterogeneous group of women than might have been thought. When asked why the romances were popular with them, the respondents gave many reasons, but a third of the replies mentioned well-written books with interesting stories and plots. A further quarter said that they were pleasant light reading. Fourteen per cent said they were relaxing or easy to read, and a further 12 per cent of replies mentioned that they were clean and wholesome or not sordid. This sort of appraisal may seem slightly naïve to the literary critic who would find one story almost indistinguishable from another and all of them highly predictable in their endings. But we are not concerned with this type of analysis here. Clearly much of the content of the light romantic novel *is* escapism, but it is clear that the readers are fully aware of the escapism in the books and this is one of their attractions. The books are well written of their kind and the reader is able to 'get into' them quite quickly. In some cases readers say 'once you start reading them you can't stop until you reach the end.' In other cases readers say how easy they are to put down and pick up again. Many readers noted that they were able to 'lose themselves' in the stories and identify with the heroines. Reading in bed was clearly a common practice. Quite a number of the popular authors write books with foreign backgrounds and these are popular with housewives and such people whose opportunities of world-wide travel are limited. Heroes are often masterful and always interesting; frequently they are quite rude to the heroine on initial acquaintance, but this seems to add spice to the story. Against some popular misconceptions, 'slushy' romance is clearly *not* popular at all, but equally violence is not wanted and the 'kitchen-sink' format is not welcomed by women who spend hours at the real thing. The readers *want* a form of fantasy in their reading; they have the reality of a woman's role every day and they look to the romances for unreality. Mills & Boon advertise their romantic novels as 'pleasant' books. One woman wrote, 'They are clean and wholesome without any unpleasant sexy stuff. They all leave one with a satisfactory sense of pleasant and hopeful existence. I find them cheerful and relaxing.' This quotation sums up a lot of the readers' views.

The romantic novel, as studied in this survey, turns out to be a form of book which has a wide variety of readers, many of whom use this type of book for different sorts of functions. For some it is clearly a fairy-tale escape from nappies and sinks; for others it is a mental unwinding after a day of hard concentration. But whatever the satisfaction gained by women of different ages, occupations, education and marital status it is clear that for all of them (and numerically these readers are quite important) *reading books* is a favoured form of leisure activity. The ability to read a full 200-page novel depends on a certain degree of literacy. The desire to read such a novel can only be stimulated by good authors helped on by efficient publishers and distributors. To judge this part of the book reading world by the highest standards of literary criticism is an error; to despise it for its simplicity is arrogance.

Chapter 6

Conclusions

This book has ranged widely over a number of studies carried out with the object of looking at the place of books in people's lives. If there is any one single conclusion that can be made at the end of such a diversified study it is that the book is still very much a part of people's lives in our modern society, and in spite of television, radio, film and the newly invented audio-visual cassettes intended to be played through people's television sets, the book in its ordinary conventional form is still the most important means of communication ever invented. McLuhan may believe that things are changing, but for sheer versatility in catering for people's interests from work to pure leisure the book is still of prime importance in people's lives.

Having said this, it must be recognised that books do not play a large part directly in everyone's lives. All of us *must* have quite a lot to do with books during our years of formal education and it is noteworthy that even before formal education begins parents are proud when their children show early signs of ability in reading. Indeed, such is the status derived from early reading ability that some parents push their children too fast and build up antagonisms to reading in them. But at school the child who is at ease with books, who comes from a home where books are a *normal* part of living (not just unused status objects or talismans, such as educational encyclopedia so often are) and who lives in a family where words are used and enjoyed, that child is half way towards success in the educational system which seeks to teach the child to learn from others and to communicate with others. And it is through the book that so much of this communication takes place because the book has a permanency no other medium has, and it has an individuality in communication which is quite unique.

By individuality of communication is meant that essential privacy shared between the reader and the book that no other means of communication can provide. It is significant that we use phrases such as 'being lost in a book' or 'inside a book' which suggest that the reader is actually somehow a part of the book he is reading. One cannot imagine a reviewer being lost in a television set or even caught in the pages of a magazine. Book reading has an intimacy which no other communication has and it is not equalled by newspapers or magazines which, too, use the printed word.

For these reasons books are special, books are different. Doubtless psychologists of the Freudian school could suggest that books are womb substitutes, but on a less clinical level the book can be seen as a unique object with which the personal connection is very important. Why is it that some people develop such special feelings about books that they spend large portions of their income in buying them and stocking them all around their homes? Why do some people find it almost impossible to throw away even the most dog-eared and tattered old books which they know should go into the dust-bin? Why are these paper objects put away in attics, cupboards or spare bedrooms where no one will ever use them again simply because the owners cannot bear to part with them? Many people have hoarding instincts for things like pieces of string or paper clips, but the hoarding instinct for books is not only acknowledged by our society, it is even applauded.

Yet, as everyone knows, it is possible to live a completely happy life while having an absolute minimum contact with books. The public libraries will provide us with any book we want, albeit we may have to wait some time if our library is only a small one or our needs are very special. But inter-library loans will bring virtually any book in print to the borrower, given sufficient time. Even so, many people can still get along quite happily without even needing to borrow books. In their lives their leisure relaxation is met by cinema, radio and television, media which use the spoken word and the projected image. For their hobbies and their practical interests these people find newspapers and magazines give them all the written information they feel they want. The book is just not necessary for them. They are the people one sees on train journeys who can sit, apparently quite happily, for hours *not* reading at all. They are the people we see in the doctors waiting room who sit patiently just looking ahead and doing nothing whilst the rest of us read the paperbacks we had slipped in our pockets before we left home or mull over the ancient magazines so kindly provided free of charge by the GP who is keeping us waiting. It must be accepted that books are special, but not special for everybody, and the problem is that once people move out of the world of books which they are exposed to at school they frequently find that books are not necessary for them. It could be argued that, put this way, a value judgment rather than a statement of fact is being advanced. For the person who does enjoy books it is bound to seem a cultural lack when other people do not care about books, and in this case a judgment is being made. But it is a fact that people who live without books live outside a great deal of the cultural heritage of their society and they are also cut off from large areas of knowledge and contemporary affairs and scientific and technical knowledge. So being without books is, in some ways, a form of cultural deprivation, albeit that this deprivation is self-chosen.

It has already been said that contact with books often ceases when people complete their full-time education, and it must be recognised that for some young people books are inextricably bound up with an education which they have not enjoyed and which they are happy to be finished with. Children of lesser intelligence and those who are poor readers anyway can be expected to react against 'book learning' because of their own inferiorities. But many children of reasonable intelligence and ability do not come to enjoy using books because the part that books play in their lives is not an exciting or stimulating one. The dirty, dog-eared, broken-spined and microscopic print copies of the so-called 'classics' of English literature which are still handed out at the beginning of each school year to our children are a damning indictment of educational mis-spending and they help produce yet another generation for whom 'literature' means any author who is now mercifully dead but who wrote at unending length when he or she was alive. But books are more than just 'literature', they are information, advice, 'know-how' and the references children need for many activities. If books are seen as tools

178

for living then they fulfil a host of functions, from the young girl who wants a simple cookery book to begin her first experiments with buns and cakes to the young man who wants an authoritative yet readable manual on how to tune his two-stroke engine. Books are information, but information is only of value when it is readily available for the person who wants or needs it. The problem, and the tragedy, is that our society makes such poor use of the books that it has. Our children in schools and even our adolescents and young adults in colleges are assumed to have a natural wish to use books and a natural instinct for finding their way around classification systems and catalogues. The *use* of books is rarely regarded with any seriousness in our educational institutions. Librarianship as a *teaching* function is only just beginning slowly to percolate through. At present school librarians are still trying to overcome the sloth and backwardness of decades, and school librarians who are not teachers are still regarded as rather low-grade clerical assistants. But with the development of large comprehensive schools the light is gradually beginning to dawn and more thought is now being given to libraries as places where pupils come to *use* books, rather than as the room where the books are kept to stop the pupils getting at them.

With the spread of higher education more and more young people are entering universities and recent figures have shown that approximately 200,000 young people are at university in this country. Their libraries provide them with some of the finest collections of books in the country, yet education for the use of these libraries is often rudimentary if it exists at all. The first-week-of-term-show-around is pathetically inadequate for young people who may be expected, as in the arts and social sciences, to spend twenty or more hours a week in the library. And as collections grow and university libraries split up into large sub-sections their complexity will grow all the more. The need for library education in the higher realms of education is becoming very pressing.

But young people in universities are expected to buy books as well as to borrow them. Each normal student grant includes £38 per annum to provide for books and stationery. If we allow £6 for stationery then £32 is left for books. Yet the surveys of student expenditure on books give an average of £12 a year actually spent. So if we multiply the unused £20 by the 200,000 students the result is £4 million a year given to students by the tax- and rate-payers which is not spent on buying books. Here clearly is a misappropriation of public funds on a vast scale, yet the answer, which could be by means of book vouchers, would undoubtedly be political dynamite and would undoubtedly be claimed by student leaders to be just another threat to the freedom which is so dear to them (yet even dearer to the tax-payer). But we are not here so much concerned with the economics of the student non-book-buying. What is relevant to this study is the clearly apparent lack of *desire* to buy books which this misuse of student grants demonstrates. Placed in the highest educational institutions of the land, with university bookshops at their doorsteps and provided with the money to buy books, the students do not want to buy. Some lecturers would doubtless add that some of them do not want to borrow or even to read, but the essential point is that even at university the lack of feeling for books is demonstrated in a devastating way to the tune of £4 million a year of books not bought.

And so, even with the spread of higher education, there is still a strong antipathy to be overcome if young people with the highest levels of education are to become at ease with books. These young people are the ones who might be expected to be accustomed to using books as a normal part of their lives. For less well-educated people whose work necessitates little contact with books their disinclination to borrow or buy is much more easily understandable.

It is very difficult to study what people do *not* do since surveys of people's non-activities raise great difficulties for the interviewer. During the programme of research reported in this book an attempt was made to study the non-reader, but it was on too limited a scale and the results were inconclusive. There is, however, a real need for a better understanding of the non-reader since an understanding of the lives of people who get along quite happily without books would be valuable complementary information to place alongside the increasing knowledge we now have of the reader. Such a study of the non-reader would be arduous and would require interviewing skills of a high order coupled with a tenacity on the part of the interviewers to overcome the many dispiriting refusals by people disinclined to talk to a stranger about something they are not interested in. But if it were possible to carry out a full-scale study of the non-reader the results would undoubtedly be of great value to educationalists, to librarians and to the whole of the book trade. It is also certain that the study of the non-reader would have to deal with such people's leisure interests which exclude reading and so a better understanding would be gained of general leisure activities in our society, a field of enquiry which is only now beginning to attract the belated attention of a small number of sociologists.

The field of leisure reading is an important one, as the library survey in this book has shown. The study of the readers of Mills & Boon romances is, so far as is known, unique, but it would be extremely valuable to know something about the male equivalents – the readers of the 'men's romances' which are normally of a lower moral tone and would cover all the brightly covered breast-sellers so attractively displayed in bookshops of all types and also on bookstalls, in newsagents and so on. Again it would be difficult to carry out such a study since sampling is difficult, but research has already been initiated into the *general* purchases of paperbacks in the Opinion Research Centre paperback survey which is carried out at quarterly intervals, and so an *ad hoc* survey on similar lines using a national sample of 'retail outlets' is possible, though clearly the costs would be relatively high. But pilot studies on a smaller scale in a small number of selected places would be valuable enough to produce some impressions which could be used for further large-scale research if this were felt to be justified by the initial pilot results. It is surprising that the sales of light fiction, particularly in paperback form, are so large and form such an important part of the book trade, and yet no research has yet been carried out into the consumers of these products.

A further section of books which could warrant further study are those in the 'model' which come under the heading of 'home manuals and reference'. The surveys have indicated that many people who may be regarded as being on the fringe of book culture do use books quite a lot for their hobbies and practical interests. This is an important category since it is here that books can be appreciated for their usefulness and where books can be regarded as tools of living which do not frighten or intimidate people who would find 'books as literature' overpowering. This section of books is very important since (as publishers well know) successful books in this field can be genuine best sellers with very large sales over a long period of time compared to the so-called Sunday paper best sellers which may have a brief hour of glory but no staying power. The home manuals and similar reference books are important to both librarians and booksellers since they cater for needs which transcend social classes and help bring more people into the libraries and bookshops because people genuinely feel a *need* (as against a mere want) for books on quite practical subjects. One does not have to be in the literary swim to appreciate one's need of a good book on gardening, or car maintenance, or on making puppets, and a visit to a bookshop or library for such needs carries no problems of social status with it. These utilitarian books can thus be regarded as useful baits to lure people into the libraries and bookshops, and if their needs are well catered for there then the barriers which exist in people's minds may be broken down.

But all the suggestions that have been made above require energy, thought, coordination of effort and, of course, the expenditure of time and money. One of the greatest problems for everyone concerned in the world of books is to get through to people who are marginal to or quite outside the world of books, the fact that books are for people and are for all the people, because whatever a person's interests or needs may be, somewhere in the great pile of a quarter of a million titles in print there will be a suitable book for him. To steal from the GPO advertising theme – 'Somewhere, someplace, there is a book waiting for you.' The problem is to link the book to the person and such is the great range of books and so many are the people that putting the two together in individual cases is a tremendous exercise in communication. There is no doubt that libraries are now much more aware than they were of the information needs of their readers and in Chapter 1 mention was made of some excellent examples. The Library Association and the National Book League, at national levels, both produce valuable bibliographical material. But the problem is that so often, even at the local library or bookshop level, the preaching is to the converted. It was reported at the Booksellers Association Conference in 1970 that Hudson's bookshop in Birmingham had, very enterprisingly, a general 'Christmas gifts' catalogue delivered to people's homes late in 1969, but the results had not been very good and this drop in the ocean seemed too small and not effective enough to justify the financial outlay.

So the problem of communication remains the greatest one of all. Right from the university student with his unspent £20 a year (who may well put it to other uses because his lecturers give him too little guidance on what to buy and merely bewilder him with great lists of 'recommended readings' which would take a lifetime to cover) across to the complete non-reader who is quite happy in his world without books, there are great numbers of people whose lives could be fuller and more satisfying were they brought into better contact with books of all types.

There have been people in recent years who have viewed with gloom the future prospects of the book. Undoubtedly there will be great advances in the years to come of mechanical and electrical teaching devices, information retrieval with tele-printing on demand, micro-photographing, audio-visual cassettes and so on. All these will have their part in increasing man's access to knowledge. Entertainment media will undoubtedly develop in technological complexity and it may well be that we shall be able to have home printed news-sheets from our television sets. But nothing which has yet been suggested in this range of twentieth-century marvels seems to provide the satisfactions which the book gives. Whether it is the well-thumbed reference book in study, workshop or kitchen, whether it is the biography or the novel borrowed from the library, or whether it is the personal copy always there on one's own bookshelves, the book is a *private* medium of communication in a world where privacy is becoming more difficult to attain and maintain. Other media of communication may have their attractions but for many people a world without books would be an Orwellian nightmare, and the importance of freedom to read in the permanent form of the book is one of the freedoms which distinguishes the truly free societies of this world from the totalitarian ones, no matter how the latter may describe themselves. If the future of society is to bring with it an enlargement of man's interests and of his intellectual development books must have a key place in that world.

APPENDIX 1
DILLON'S UNIVERSITY BOOKSHOP SURVEY

This visit:

1. Why have you just been to Dillons? (PROMPT if need: Tick all)

   (1) To buy from stock ☐ (2) To collect an order ☐   I

   (3) To have a look round ☐ (4) Passing by ☐

   (5) To enquire about an order ☐ (6) To meet someone ☐

   (7) Other, specify...

2. Did you buy or order anything? (Include collecting order: Tick all)

   (1) Bought book(s) sought ☐ (2) Bought book(s) on impulse   2

   (3) Collected order ☐ (4) Order not arrived ☐

   (5) Ordered book(s) ☐ (6) Bought book token(s) ☐

   (7) Nothing bought ☐ (8) Other ....

---

3. How many books in all have you bought? .... None ☐   3

   What were their prices? Intended/Impulse. Book token=BT

Intended	Impulse

   Enter prices under headings

4
5
6
7
8
9

---

4. Can you tell me what departments of the shop you have just visited?

   (PROMPT OR AID if need: Tick all)

   (1) .... (2)   10

186

(3) ....   (4)   11

(5) ....   (6)   12

(7) ....   (8) ....

5. How long were you in the shop altogether? ....mins.   13

About Dillons in General

6. (a) Would you call Dillons your *main* London bookshop?

      Yes ☐   No ☐   D.K. ☐   14

   (b) If NO or D.K., what is your main London bookshop?

      None ☐   Name..............................   15

   (c) Do you use any bookshop outside London regularly?

      Yes ☐   No ☐

      If YES, Who? Where?.............................   16

7. About how long have you been a customer at Dillons?   17

     Not applic. ☐   Under 1 year ☐   .... years

8. Do you buy the books you use for your work or study from Dillons?

   PROMPT   Not. applic. ☐   18

   All ☐   Most ☐   Some ☐   Few ☐   None ☐

9. Do you buy your books that are not connected with your work from Dillons?   PROMPT   Not applic. ☐   19

   All ☐   Most ☐   Some ☐   Few ☐   None ☐

10. Do you ever buy second-hand books from Dillons?   PROMPT

   Often ☐   Sometimes ☐   Rarely ☐   Never ☐   N.K. ☐   20

11. Do you ever buy antiquarian books from Dillons?   PROMPT

   Often ☐   Sometimes ☐   Rarely ☐   Never ☐   N.K. ☐   21

12. Do you ever buy books as presents for other people from Dillons?

   PROMPT

   Often ☐   Sometimes ☐   Rarely ☐   Never ☐   Not. applic. ☐   22

13. Do you ever buy book tokens from Dillons? PROMPT
    Often ☐ Sometmes ☐ Rarely ☐ Never ☐ Not applic. ☐   23

14. Can you suggest any ways in which Dillons could be improved,
    for example

    (a) The stock of books?.....................................   24
      25

    (b) The layout of the shop?...............................   26
      27

15. About the staff: (a) Have you ever asked a member of the staff
    for help?   Yes ☐   No ☐   28

    If YES, would you say the staff in general are helpful or unhelpful?
    Helpful ☐   Unhelpful ☐   No opinion ☐   29

    Record any comment...................................   30
    (b) Do you think the staff are easy to find or not? Yes ☐ No☐ 31
    Record any comment   32

    (c) How do you think the standard of service could be improved? 33
      34
    ....

16. Do you know any bookshops that you think are better than
    Dillons?
    Yes ☐   No ☐   If YES, give shops and reasons   35

    (a)   36
    (b)   37
    (c)   38

17. What do you think are Dillons best points? NO PROMPT   39
      40

18. Do you ever see any advertisements for Dillons – in magazines for
    example?
    Yes ☐   No ☐   If YES, where?   41

    ....

19. Have you seen a Dillons catalogue of any sort this autumn?
    Yes ☐   No ☐   42

    If YES, which one(s) and how did you obtain it (them)?   43
      44

20. Do you have an account at Dillons? Yes ☐ No ☐ Did once ☐   45

Now just a few questions about yourself

21. Are you a student?   Full-time ☐   Part-time ☐   No ☐   46

    IF A STUDENT (Full or Part-time)

22. What college (or other institution)?..........................   47

23. What course are you on?................................   48

24. What year of study? ...... U.G. ☐ P.G. ☐ Not. applic. ☐   49

25. Where do you live in term time?........... Tick Home ☐   50

26. Where is your home town (if different)?......................   51

27. About how much do you expect to spend on books this academic
    year? £........   52

28. What is your *basic* L.E.A. grant? £........   Not applic.   53

    IF NOT A FULL-TIME STUDENT

29 What is your occupation?................................   54

30. What firm do you work for?..............................   55

31. What is your place of work?..............................   56

32. Where did you complete your full-time education?..........   57

    ALL RESPONDENTS

33. Sex (1) Male ☐   (2) Female ☐   58

34. Age (1) Under 21 ☐   (2) 21–24 ☐

     (3) 25–34 ☐   (4) 35–44 ☐   59

     (5) 45–54 ☐   (6) 55–64 ☐

     (7) 65 and over ☐

35. Martial status (1) Single ☐   (2) Married ☐

     (3) Widowed ☐   (4) Divorced ☐   60

     (5) Married student apart ☐

36. Nationality   British born ☐   Others.............. 61

Day of interview   M Tu W Th F S   Ring   62
Interview began..............a.m./p.m.   Ended......a.m./p.m.
Interviewer's initials..............

APPENDIX 2

A. B. WARD BOOKSHOP SURVEY

This visit
  1. Why have you just visited the bookshop? (multiple code)

☐ To buy a particular title
☐ To buy a certain kind of book
☐ To buy any book
☐ To have a general look around
☐ To enquire about an order
☐ To collect an order
☐ To exchange a book token
☐ Other, please specify ....
☐ No answer

  2. Did you in fact buy anything? (multiple code)
☐ Nothing bought
☐ Bought book(s) sought
☐ Collected order
☐ Bought book(s) on impulse
☐ Bought book token
☐ Other please specify ....
☐ No answer

  3. How many books in all have you bought? .... ☐ None

People intending to buy, but made no purchase
  4. I see you were looking for a book and you didn't buy anything. Can you tell me why not?

☐ Not in stock
☐ Couldn't find the kind of thing I wanted
☐ Other, please specify ....
☐ No answer

  5. Did you make an order? ☐ Yes ☐ No

If books were bought

6. For each: What is its title?

7.   Did you intend buying it?

8.   What is its price?

9, 10.   Is it for yourself, or someone else? Who?

11.   Is it for work a hobby, or to be read for leisure?

12.   Did you find it yourself or ask an assistant?

| Title | Mark Price | | Self | Other | Who? | Work | Hobby | Leisure | Self | Asst. |
	Intended	Impulse								

For all customers

13. Which kinds of books did you look at?

1	2
3	4
5	6
7	8

14. Did you come in to town especially to visit Wards, or was it part of other shopping . . . or on the way home from work?

    ☐ Special visit

    ☐ Part of other shopping

    ☐ Dropped in from work

    ☐ Other, please specify . . . .

Buying books generally

15. How often do you come to Wards?

    ☐ A Once a week or more frequently

    ☐ B Once or twice a month

    ☐ C Once or twice in six months

    ☐ D Less frequently than that

    ☐ E First visit

16. Do you buy books from anywhere else (PROMPT, IF NECESSARY)

    ☐ Yes   ☐ No

17. *If yes*, where and how often do you go there?

Name of Shop	A	B	C	D

18. About how many books have you bought in the last year? . . . .

19. What kind of books are they mainly?

. . . .
. . . .
. . . .
. . . .

20. When did you start buying books?

    ....
    ....
    ....
    ....

21. Do many of your friends buy books?

    ☐ Most   ☐ Some   ☐ Few   ☐ None   ☐ No answer

    Comments (NO PROMPT) ....
    ....

22. Do the following people in your family buy books?

	What kind of books?	*Often*	*Some-times*	*Rarely*	*Never*
Father					
Mother					
Husband/ Wife					
Children					

23. Do you ever give books as presents? What kind? To whom?

    (Record comments) ....
    ....
    ....
    ....

24. Do you ever receive books as presents? What kind? From whom?

    (Record comments) ....
    ....
    ....
    ....

25. Do you belong to a public library?

    ☐ Yes   ☐ No   ☐ Used to

26. Do you visit it ☐ Weekly or fortnightly

    ☐ Every two months or so

    ☐ Once or twice a year

27. What kind of books do you borrow mainly?

    ....

    ....

    ....

28. Can you name any book which you have bought after borrowing it from the library?

    ....

    ....

29. Do you associate bookshops with any particular kinds of people? (NO PROMPT)

    ....

    ....

    ....

30. Which of the following statements describes best your attitude to bookshops? (USE PROMPT CARD)

31. Do you belong, or have you ever belonged to a book club?

    ☐ Yes

    ☐ Used to   } Which one? ....

    ☐ No

Personal Details

32. What is your occupation?..

33. Where is your place of work? ....

34. (If possible) What firm do you work for? ....

35. Where did you complete your full-time education? ....
....

36. Have you done, or are you doing any evening class or correspondence course?

☐ Evening class ☐ Correspondence course

☐ Yes

☐ Have done

☐ No

37. *If a student*, what college ....
☐ Full-time ☐ Part-time

38. Sex ☐ Male ☐ Female

39. Age ☐ Under 16 ☐ 35–44

☐ 16–20 ☐ 45–54

☐ 21–24 ☐ 55–64

☐ 25–34 ☐ 65+

APPENDIX 3
SHEFFIELD LIBRARY SURVEY, 1969

This visit
1. Could you tell me why you have just visited the library?

   ☐ To return books

   ☐ To return and borrow books

   ☐ To borrow books

   ☐ To look something up

   ☐ To return/borrow gramophone records

   ☐ Other, specify ....

If books were borrowed (for each)
2. What was the title?

3. Was it a title you wanted specifically, a certain type of book (or subject) or was it just 'something to read'?

4. Is it for yourself, or someone else? Who?

5. Is the book for work, for a hobby, or leisure reading?
   (Check .... books borrowed)

Title	Specific title	Specific Subject	Some-thing to read	Self	Other	Who	Work	Hobby	Leisure

197

6. Did you come in to borrow any books which you were not able to find?

☐ Yes What? ....

☐ No

7. If any of the books were 'just to read,' could you tell me how you went about choosing these books?

....
....
....

8. Did you consult the assistants about anything? ☐ Yes ☐ No

If yes, record details

....
....

9. Did you use the catalogue at all ☐ Yes ☐ No

If yes, What for? Record details...........................

....

10. Which sections of the library did you visit?

1	2
3	4
5	6
7	8
9	10

11. How long were you in the library altogether? ....minutes

12. Did you come into town specially to visit the library or was it part of other shopping. . . or was it on the way from work, etc.?

☐ Special visit

☐ Part of other shopping

☐ Lunch-hour

☐ On the way to or from work

☐ Other, please specify ....

Using the library generally

13. How often do you visit the library? (PROMPT)

    ☐ More than once a week

    ☐ Weekly or fortnightly

    ☐ Every month or so

    ☐ About once every three months

    ☐ Once every six months

    ☐ Less frequently than this

14. Do you ever use a branch library or mobile van?

    ☐ No   ☐ Branch   ☐ Van

    How often? ....

15. How many books do you usually borrow? ....

16. What kind of books are they mainly? (PROMPT)

    ....
    ....
    ....

17. When did you begin to use a Public Library?

    ....
    ....
    ....

18. Can you remember anyone suggesting it to you?

    ....
    ....
    ....
    ....

19. Do many of your friends use the library?

    ☐ Most   ☐ Some   ☐ A few   ☐ None   ☐ No answer

    Record any comments (NO PROMPT) ....
    ....

20. Do the following people in your family use the library?

	What kind of book?	Often	Some-time	Rarely	Never
Father					
Mother					
Husband/Wife					
Children					

21. Do you associate libraries with particular kinds of people? (NO PROMPT)
   ....
   ....
   ....

22. Which of these statements describes best your attitude to libraries?
   (USE PROMPT CARD)

23. Do you ever buy books? ☐ Yes ☐ No

24. *If yes*, what kind are they mainly? ....
   ....
   ....

25. How many have you bought in the last year? ....
   (Include paperbacks and gifts)

26. Do you ever give books as gifts? What kind? To whom?
   (record comments) ....
   ....
   ....

27. Do you ever receive books as gifts? What kind? From whom?
   (record comments) ....
   ....
   ....

Personal Details

28. What is your occupation? ....

29. Where is your place of work? ....

30. (If possible) What firm do you work for? ....

31. Where did you complete your full time education? ....

    ....

32. Have you done, or are you doing any evening class or correspondence course?

    ☐ Evening class   ☐ Correspondence course

    ☐ Yes   ☐ Have done   ☐ No

33. *If a student*, what college?

    ☐ Full-time   ☐ Part-time

34. Sex   ☐ Male   ☐ Female

35. Age   ☐ Under 16   ☐ 35–44

           ☐ 16–20   ☐ 45–54

           ☐ 21–24   ☐ 55–64

           ☐ 25–34   ☐ 65+

Index